Prai

"Spurvey has a uniqu and focusing on gratitude, shifting attitude, and using a cycle of success, his emphasis on a vision shift can help anyone looking to refocus on success."

—MANDY WOODLAND, LAWYER, WWW.MANDYWOODLANDLAW.COM

"While Spurvey's intent was to write a book targeted at sales, I think he has gone much further. It certainly doesn't read like a book about sales. Yet it embraces the new philosophies that people need to consider in order to be successful in sales today."

—JOEL SWEENEY, OWNER, PROFESSIONALLY SPEAKING,
WWW.JOELSWEENEY.COM

"Spurvey doesn't *tell* you lessons of a life in sales, he brings you along the journey with him so that you experience it, internalize it, and grow from it."

—SAM BROMLEY, MANAGING DIRECTOR,
WHITECAP SCIENTIFIC CORPORATION, WWW.ROV3D.COM

"Not your typical business book, *It's Time to Sell* will captivate you and inspire you at the same time. Chris has relayed his knowledge of and talent for sales in a way that's easy to read and absorb. This book has changed my outlook on business and how I approach selling."

—CHRIS DUFF, REALTOR, WWW.CHRISDUFF.CA

"*It's Time to Sell* changed my perspective on selling and challenged my thinking about what I've read from other sales and self-help authors. I began to look at not only my career but also my personal life in a different light. *It's Time to Sell* is a must-read for today's sales professionals and for all professionals in today's uber-competitive work environment."

—LESLIE PENNEY, GENERAL MANAGER AND SENIOR MORTGAGE BROKER,
MORTGAGE ALLIANCE PROVINCIAL MORTGAGE GROUP,
WWW.MORTGAGEALLIANCE.COM/LESLIEPENNEY

IT'S TIME TO SELL

IT'S TIME TO SELL

Cultivating the
SALES MIND-SET

CHRIS
SPURVEY

For information about this title or to order other books and/or electronic media, contact the publisher:

Chris Spurvey

www.chrisspurvey.com

info@chrisspurvey.com

ISBN:

Print: 978-0-9948849-0-9

eBook: 978-0-9948849-1-6

Printed in The United States of America

Cover and Interior design: 1106 Design

To my parents Hilda and Bill Spurvey—
I am the luckiest son on the planet.

CONTENTS

Visit www.chrisspurvey.com/itstimetosell
to download the free workbook accompaniment
to this book.

AUTHOR'S NOTE

What follows is a narrative based on my experiences as both student and mentor in the world of sales. I have chosen to present my vision in this form to best inspire, educate, and motivate others. Some people will want to know exactly which character I most resemble. The truth is that I am all of them—and so are you. Who you identify with may change upon subsequent readings or based on your current situation. My hope is that you will benefit from all of the content and remember your own history that has gotten you to this point even as you are inspired to take your journey ever further.

And now, let us proceed with our adventure.

ACKNOWLEDGMENTS

I am grateful to a very long list of teachers and mentors: Richard Brooke, Bob Proctor, Earl Nightingale, Robert Kiyosaki, Michelle Hyatt, Tony Robbins, Amanda Maynard, Zig Ziglar, Timothy Gallwey, Maxwell Maltz, Steven Pressfield, and Og Mandino.

I am especially grateful to Earl Nightingale and Bob Proctor, who have paved the way for so many, including me, to realize their true potential.

I would like to thank those who read the early versions of this book and offered their valuable feedback: Joel Sweeney, Adam Puddicomb, Mandy Woodland, Leslie Penney, Roger Kennedy, Sam Bromley, and Chris Duff. I will be forever grateful.

It is impossible to succeed alone, and I want to thank all who made this book a reality: my writing coach Stuart Horwitz—I enjoyed our brainstorming sessions and feel we both learned a ton from each other, my copy editor Louann Pope, and the team at 1106 Design for creating a cover that represents the nature of the book.

I appreciate all of my friends who were in my corner throughout the year I wrote this book. You know who you are.

I was fortunate to be born into the best family on the planet. My mom and dad laid a foundation that inspired me to create and continue to create the life of my dreams. They have been there to cheer me on and pick me up and dust me off when I made mistakes.

Before writing this book, I decided I wanted to write a book that my children could read and understand. Throughout the process, I kept both Parker and Anna Lili in my mind in hopes that I could create a foundation for them to grow into. I would like to thank both of them for inspiring me to write this book.

Last, but certainly not least, I would like to thank Jennifer. You are not only my wife, but also my best friend. It is humbling to look at what we have created together.

INTRODUCTION

This particular Wednesday in November had the makings to be like the year's 301 days before it. The slip of paper on which I had marked down my five goals for the year lay on my nightstand. I had been ignoring the list for the last few months, because those goals were simply reminders of how far I was from achieving them.

My wife, Nora, had supported me in my career up to this point, but I knew she was ready for me to focus on what really matters—being a loving and present husband and father. And what I needed to do in order for that to happen was to square away my work situation, once and for all.

I decided to get up. It was just before 6:00 a.m., and I knew I had one hour for quiet contemplation before the busy family routine would kick in. I walked out to the living room, fell into the recliner, turned on the gas fireplace, and just stared at the flame.

I thought about my jump into the sales profession a few years earlier. I had seen sales as a ticket to greater potential.

But while I enjoyed the client interactions and relationships, I was miserable.

You see, my boss was a numbers-game guy. If I didn't meet my targets for the number of new contacts and face-to-face meetings each month, I would miss out on a much needed bonus. The quality of the interactions didn't matter—it was all about the sheer number of contacts.

The day before, I had sat with him to review my monthly objectives, and he had denied me the bonus because my prospect had changed his appointment at the last minute, putting me one meeting under quota. With great anger and disgust, I had walked out of his office and slammed the door behind me. In fact, I had slammed the door so hard that the glass pane had shattered. This had happened at 5:00 p.m. yesterday, and I knew I would have to face the consequences today.

The thought of quitting crossed my mind, but that wasn't an option. . . . I needed the paycheck. Then it occurred to me that maybe I should stick it out and see if I could influence things toward change at the company. The owners seemed to be great people. I couldn't imagine they were happy with the way things were going. Revenues were down month after month, and my boss, the Director of Sales, didn't seem to have a handle on the business. Suddenly, optimism took root somewhere inside me. Maybe I really could influence change? After all, wasn't my vision of sales different than my boss's?

By this time it was almost 7:00 a.m. Time to get Nora and the kids up and get the day moving. I walked into the bedroom and was greeted by Nora, who gave me a supportive hug and told me that she loved me. As she embraced me, I felt this woman's love, which really was unconditional. At the same time, my eye fell on the slip of paper, still on my nightstand, that held my goals. One goal, in particular, caught my eye: attend a sales training seminar. It occurred to me that, because it was already November, I only had one month in the year left to follow through on this one. With that, my young son and daughter ran out of their rooms, diverting my attention. I went into the kitchen to make breakfast.

The day turned out to be a fairly normal one at the office. I sent my boss an apologetic email. He replied, indicating that he understood my frustration and that we would work together to get things on track. *Phew!* I thought, *I'm not fired.*

As I was going through my backlog of emails, I saw one that a buddy of mine had forwarded to me. This seemed to be his mission in life: to track down as much input as he could and disseminate it to everyone far and wide. This subject line, however, caught my attention: *It's Time to Sell.* Could it be a coincidence? Why had I noticed my goals this morning, after blocking them out for months, and why had my eye focused on that particular goal, to attend such a seminar?

I opened the e-mail and clicked the link to go to the presenter's website.

Like many salespeople I gravitate toward learning about personal development. All of that material makes total sense to me intellectually, even if I have yet to apply the principles to my own life on a consistent basis. After reading a good book or listening to a great audio recording, I find myself pumped up for a while, but before long I find myself back in the same old habits and self-talk that have gotten me where I am. What would make this event any different?

The presenter was going to do one more seminar before the end of the year, and it was this upcoming weekend in Fargo, North Dakota. The maximum number of registrants was twenty—were any seats left? I looked up Fargo, North Dakota, on the map. Because I'm from Newfoundland, Canada, some of the U.S. states are unknown territory to me. I made note that it was south of Winnipeg.

I then checked my Aeroplan frequent flyer account. I knew I could not buy a full-fare ticket, because I simply had no money. Nora and I were in debt up to our eyeballs. It was so bad that she had to call me before buying even the most basic essentials, such as clothes and school supplies for the children, to check if there was money in our bank account. We were at the end of our rope financially.

Did I have enough points? Yes, and there was one seat available on a flight that would get me into Winnipeg tomorrow night. The seminar was scheduled to start at 1 p.m. on Friday, the following day, so I would have enough time to rent a car and drive from Winnipeg to Fargo. I checked my credit card balance. I had $2,000 available credit. Surely that would be enough to pay for a rental car and hotel room.

Without thinking, I called the phone number on the presenter's website and found out there was exactly one seat remaining in the seminar. Even though I was going through troubled times and sometimes had a very negative attitude, I still believed deep down that everything happens for a reason.

I took the spot.

My flight landed in Winnipeg the next night around midnight. It was a four-hour drive down I-29 into North Dakota. I had rented a Chevy Malibu and was none too sure about its traction with a thin layer of snow on the road. The only other vehicles on the highway were semi-trailer trucks. I pulled in behind one of them and figured it would be safest to stay there in the slow lane.

I thought about the upcoming workshop with nervous anticipation. After all, I didn't know anyone. There was no guarantee that anything I would learn could be used at my current workplace; my boss and I had made up, but I didn't think he had changed his stripes.

Just then, I noticed that the red lights on the back of the rig in front of me were reflecting off the surface of the wind-swept highway. The thought crossed my mind that there may be black ice on the road. The second that thought came, the Chevy started doing multiple 360-degree spins in the middle of the highway. As I was spinning around and around in a scene that would surely end badly, I felt a calmness come over me.

It was surreal. It was as though I knew I would be fine. The rig behind me swerved to avoid smashing into me. What had lasted at most four seconds had felt like four minutes. When the Chevy finally came to a stop, it was in the proper lane facing the sign pointing toward Fargo. Without a moment to even catch my breath, I pushed on the gas pedal again and took the exit.

I reflected on the signs, the serendipity, that had led me to this point: one spot left in the seminar, just enough frequent flyer points for a free flight, one seat left on the flight that I could actually use my points toward, the necessary money available, almost to the dollar, on my credit card . . . and now a brush with death on the icy roads of North Dakota in November. I was fully open to what tomorrow may bring.

DAY ONE

Self-Motivation

I woke up this morning with a familiar feeling of dread. The one that says my life is slipping away. The one that says not to review your goals unless you want to become even more depressed.

And then I remembered where I was: in a hotel in Fargo, North Dakota. I remembered the magic of the previous night— perhaps I was meant to be here, now. Perhaps this workshop would provide some key sales strategies to help me overcome my current blocks.

The least I could do, then, was to be prepared on my end. The seminar wouldn't begin until 1 p.m., so I went down to the hotel gym and worked out. I have to confess, I always feel more on top of my game when I am energized by exercise. When I feel lean and powerful on the outside, that feeling transfers to a motivated self-confidence on the inside. Regardless of whether I am carrying a few extra pounds, a good workout propels me into the feeling that I am back on track toward accomplishing my goals.

I showered, had breakfast, and then—a rare luxury—I lay down on the bed for a meditation that turned into a short nap. I could justify this by saying that yesterday's travels had been rigorous, which of course they had, and I hadn't gotten very much sleep last night. But what I was really doing was preparing myself to receive, to be open and centered.

It was in this state of nervous optimism that I entered the meeting room that afternoon. Most of the twenty attendees of the workshop were already present, with four to five people sitting at each round table oriented toward a projection screen and lectern. The presenter did not appear to be there yet. Oh no, I thought, does this mean he is going to enter to a music and light show—the slide deck version of dry ice—so that we are all wowed by his accomplishments? I felt a little too raw to bow down to a guru, if that was his intention.

I chose a seat at the back of the room and didn't make much eye contact with the people at my left and right. The table contained the standard gear: stainless steel water pitcher, mints, and, at each place, a glass, a notepad, a pen, and a folder that bore the embossed name of the course: *It's Time to Sell*. As I got comfortable, a few more attendees trickled into the room, and then the flow of people stopped. Silently, I counted the number of people seated in the room . . . nineteen, . . . twenty, . . . twenty-one. We were one over, I guess. . . .

At that moment, the gentleman who was seated at my right stood up and addressed the room.

"Are we all here, then?"

Heads swiveled to the back to see who was speaking. The man looked like he was in his early forties. He was of above average height and well dressed in a black suit, white shirt, no tie, and black shoes. His watch was similarly subtle: a sophisticated, stainless steel timepiece that, on closer examination, I could see was a Rolex.

"Well, then, let's get started."

The man strode to the front of the room in a confident, unhurried, fashion. When he arrived at the lectern, he paused and smiled. I don't know how he did it, but in the blink of an eye he seemed to smile at each of us individually.

"Do you want to hear about me?"

No one in the room seemed to know how to answer this question.

"Do you want to hear about my successes? The way that I, as head of the sales department of a small professional services company, led it to being acquired by one of the largest companies in the world? And how I now enjoy the fruits of that labor and live a phenomenal lifestyle?

"Or do you want to hear about how I was overweight, drifting from job to job after college, always spending more than I was making?

"Or do you," here he paused for dramatic emphasis, "do you want to hear about how I changed my vision of myself from a follower whose dominant motivation was to prove my worthiness to other people, who wanted nothing more than to prove that I belonged and would do whatever I could to fit in, to a man enjoying more of what life has to offer than I ever thought possible, by changing my thoughts, my habits, and my attitude?

"The truth is, you don't want to hear about me." At this statement, the speaker chuckled. "You want to hear about you. You only want to hear about me so you can apply my insights to your own lives. So, let's get started. By a show of hands, how many of you want more success in your lives?"

Everyone raised their hands, some more reluctantly than others.

"How many of you want to learn how to do that this weekend?"

All of the hands remained in the air.

"Unfortunately, I cannot guarantee that I can deliver on either of those. But, if there is anything I know, it is that when you bring like-minded people together in the same room great things can happen."

"You may have heard something similar in the often repeated quote, 'When the student is ready, the teacher will appear.'

Well, are you ready?"

The presenter then thanked us all for coming. He noted that time was the most precious resource and that he was grateful we had invested our time to attend the seminar. As he went on to thank the organizers, I found myself thinking, *I like this guy. I like his style.* I had been worried that I would find myself exposed, having to volunteer too much about myself too soon—or worse, that I would have to hear about how great somebody else had it. His approach seemed to be neither of those.

As I tuned back in, he was explaining the rationale behind the name of the workshop: *It's Time to Sell.*

"*It's Time to Sell* is about laying the foundation, or what I call the *inner game,* for the success you desire. Throughout the seminar, we will touch on some of the *outer game* principles as well, but, without the inner game covered and integrated into your life, you will never achieve your true potential.

"Now, there are a few types of people here in this room . . ."

Uh-oh! I thought, *here we go. We're going to be divided into groups, and I'm going to feel like a fool.* But I was relieved to hear what the presenter said next.

"It is up to you which category you fall into. Hopefully, I will convert you all to category one, but you hold that final decision.

"Category one is made up of those people who are completely receptive to the information I will share with you over the next couple of days. You are an open book and ready for change. Category two is the group of people who may not yet be sold, but over the next couple of days will buy into the information and energy and will leave here with new insights and modes of operation. And, finally, there are some people in this room who have complete mental blocks: category three. In this seminar you might pretend you are interested, you might hang around outside the door and talk to people, but you won't actively participate, possibly because you are afraid to learn about the parts of you that need improving.

"What category you fall into is completely up to you. I have delivered this seminar around the world to thousands and thousands of people. It is proven. Wallace D. Wattles once said in his now famous book, *The Science of Getting Rich,* and I paraphrase: If one of you apply what I have outlined and turn your lives into the success you desire, that is proof that you all can.

"You may have heard something similar in the often repeated quote, 'When the student is ready, the teacher will appear.' Well, are you ready?"

I always dread this kind of question. Am I ready? I mean, I'm here. I traveled five thousand miles to be here, which is quite a distance, come to think of it. So I must really be ready. Ready to prove to myself and to my family that there is more to life than financial hardship and torment. I need this. Is that the same thing as being ready? Nora needs this. The kids need this. I know I need this, so I pledge I will remain as open as I possibly can. And yes, I'm going to call that ready! Bring it on.

The presenter flipped through a few slides explaining that there would be overlap among the elements of *It's Time to Sell.* Words like **desire, success,** and **gratitude** flashed across the screen.

"But first we will lay the foundation for the remaining sessions. And that foundation begins with **self-motivation.**

"To achieve success in life, you need to have a high level of self-motivation. Have you ever felt unstoppable? Have you ever been in the zone? Most people at one point or another in their lives have hit a sweet spot. Perhaps you have experienced this during athletic competition . . . or while creating something artistic . . . or even while counseling a friend about a problem. You have no fear, and you know you can do no wrong. Perhaps you have recent memories in business of hitting the sweet spot?

"Self-motivation is a beautiful concoction of energy, enthusiasm, creativity, and persistence. It comes together when you feel that you have just enough of all these elements to battle through anything.

"Now, everyone has moments of self-motivation, but is it sustainable? The foundation of achieving the success you desire is building up the right level of self-motivation to break through the barriers that lay before you. How do you obtain this perfect and sustainable level of self-motivation? You need to fall in love with a vision for your life.

"A vision is a clear picture in your mind's eye of you being, doing, and having what you desire."

I thought to myself that I'd heard this before, but then I said, *Hold on. I vowed I would be open. Let's answer the question. Do I have a vision? Do I really know what that word means?*

"Think about this," the presenter continued, "If you had a clear picture in your mind of what you were working toward for your life, would you let a coworker who called you out in a meeting stand in your way? Would you let a prospect who decided your service was not for her stand in your way? Would you let the fact that your company's revenues last month were not what you had budgeted stand in your way?

"I am here to tell you that you would not. This seminar is about finding out what you desire in life, forming a clear mental picture of the life that you desire, and pouring forth the right level of consistent self-motivation to make it happen."

There seemed to be a lot of collective deep breaths in the room at that moment. The presenter went over the trajectory of the weekend's topics, but my mind was on overload.

A vision. . . . To achieve success is self-motivation. . . . What brings you self-motivation is the vision of yourself doing, having, and being everything you desire. . . . What do I desire? I mean, really?

I was grateful when the presenter called for a brief break so I could contemplate this weighty concept for possibly the first time in my life.

My mind went back to a time at the end of university when I was overweight. My condition on the outside reflected my reality on the inside: I was not happy. A friend of mine gave me a set of audio recordings designed to improve my personal power. I listened to them religiously. I set my alarm clock every day for 5:00 a.m. and heard every word of the recordings. Intellectually, the content made total sense to me: Change your thoughts and beliefs in order to change your life. I understood the theory, and it produced a moment of motivation. But, although I understood it with my conscious mind, I did not internalize it. It did not change my subconscious mind or the picture I had of myself. Yes, over a period of two months I lost fifty pounds, but I was focused entirely on the scale, on the results. So when I saw the number on the scale decreasing from 270 to 255, to 244, to 220, I did not change the vision I had in my head of who I was. And so, within two years, I gained back all of the weight.

My vision of myself was still the old one, and it was to this vision that I gravitated back over time.

Chapter 1 Summary and Reflective Questions: Self-Motivation

The foundation for success in sales begins with self-motivation.

Self-motivation is a concoction of energy, enthusiasm, creativity, and persistence.

Everyone has moments of self-motivation, but is it sustainable?

How do you obtain this perfect and sustainable level of self-motivation? You need to fall in love with a vision for your life.

A vision is a clear picture in your mind's eye of you being, doing, and having what you desire.

Desire

As we gathered back in the meeting room after the break, I stole a few looks at the individuals around me. They appeared so diverse! I didn't know what I had expected. Perhaps a narrow age range of men dressed in suits and ties? But here were women as well as men, professionals, retirees, and even a very young couple who looked like they were just out of college.

The presenter began the next segment as if he were reading my mind.

"We are all brought up in unique environments. Some of us might have experienced particularly traumatic life events that hold us back. Some of us have more fertile ground to work with. Regardless of your life history, however, I am here to tell you that it can be another way. Of course, past events have had a huge impact on your past, but that impact is created almost entirely by your creative interpretations of those past events. You each have your own personal choice to make about how those events will affect your future.

"How do you get over—or reframe—your past? It starts with a burning desire for something more. A large percentage of people don't have any idea that we are all masters of our own destiny. Or, as Thomas Carlyle once said, 'someone without a goal is like a ship without a rudder.' Now, I'm not necessarily talking about anyone in this room, but the people you meet in shops and on the road, at social gatherings and at work, do they have a goal? Do they realize what it is?

"A much smaller percentage of individuals realize life can be a lot more fruitful. They are driven by the desire to grow, to have, and to be something more. That is what this seminar is about. I am here to help you achieve that desire, because that is what success is all about: forming a vision and allowing your vision to propel you forward."

Part of me wondered again if I had heard all of this before. Then I paused, realizing that these type of thoughts were part of a defense mechanism preventing the marrow of the content from seeping into my bones. So what if I had heard some of this before? Had it done the trick? Had I been able to change my life? Not yet. Maybe I needed to hear it one more time.

I closed my eyes and reflected on desire. Could I feel that desire? It seemed that all I knew right now was necessity, born of my somewhat dire straits. Yet, at the same time, I knew the desire was there, because I didn't want to dial down my life, to start slashing the opportunities for my wife, family, or myself and get by with less. Instead, I wanted to reach up and forward, to make decisions based not on being reactive but on being proactive.

"Everyone in this room," the presenter continued, "belongs to that group of people who have decided that they can do, be, and have more. It is this desire that has brought you here. All forward-looking achievement starts with this desire for change.

"Now, as I said earlier, I could stir up your desire by telling my personal story of moving from hardship to greatness. I could wow you with pictures of my homes, drop the names of influential people who seek out my wisdom, or describe my charitable giving in a way that might inspire your desire, but all of that might also backfire and create jealousy—or worse, separation between us—in which you believe that I can reach these grand achievements but you cannot.

"That is not why I am here. I am here to help open up your mind to the fact that life can be another way and struggle is not necessary. So, I ask you, 'What do you desire to be, do, or have?'

"That most of you are, directly or indirectly, in the sales profession is evidence that you desire more. The sales profession and entrepreneurship are generally the two routes traveled by people who desire unlimited potential. Sales is a great profession. We'll talk later about whether you believe that and to what degree. For right now, we can simply say our economy does not move without the efforts of salespeople.

"So, would you agree that you desire more?"

There were some murmurs from the audience.

"And what you desire—I am willing to bet—can be summarized as more success, but what is success? Let us not take our immediate perception of 'success.' Rather, let's dissect what success really is."

Chapter 2 Summary and Reflective Questions: Desire

How do you get over—or reframe—your past?
Start with a burning desire for something more.

What past event has had a large effect on your life?

When you dissect the event, can you see that how you interpreted the event has had a large effect on you?

What do you desire to be, do, or have?

Success

After another brief break, we returned to the meeting room, only this time we found the tables rearranged into a broad semicircle around the lectern. The intent seemed to be to draw us closer together as a group, which resonated with the way the presenter then addressed us in this next segment of the workshop.

First, we were instructed to each write down our vision of success in a one-sentence statement without judgment of ourselves or of others who would eventually share their descriptions: What did we consider success? Or, if it was easier, who did we consider successful, and why?

In one sentence? I confess I was a little stuck. I kept seeing my cousin Susan in my mind. She is a doctor, so she is obviously very successful. Why did I think that? Was it a kind of subliminal message that had been planted in my subconscious mind during childhood and that now determined how I viewed success? Was it just cultural baggage? Or did I envy her because of the trips she and her family were able to take and the money I imagined she had in the bank? Hopefully, my reasoning wasn't as shallow as pointing to the fact that she could call a restaurant and make dinner reservations as a doctor!

When the presenter began calling for volunteers to deliver their one sentence statements, I had a page full of scribbles, none of which I was very proud of. I had spent the whole time comparing myself to someone else. It was almost as if I were incapable of looking at my life on its own terms.

"Okay," the presenter began, "let's see what success means to you. Now, no self-editing! Who's our first guinea pig?"

A woman who appeared to be in her late thirties or early forties started us off, saying, "I just want to be happy!"

The guru asked her, "How will you know when you are happy?"

The woman thought about it for a moment. "Because the mundane activities of day-to-day life with my family won't get to me as much once I commit to living life more proactively rather than reactively."

"Excellent!" the presenter cried. "Who's next?"

A larger man in his mid-fifties raised his hand. "I would like to have freedom from the rat race I find myself in."

"So you may mean time freedom?" the presenter asked. "And you imagine that time freedom will give you other kinds of opportunities to pursue success?"

"Yes, exactly. So I can take care of my health for the future." He rubbed his obviously large belly. "I want to be here for my kids' kids, but right now all I seem to be able to find the time for is work."

"Okay, that's a great idea of success. One more?"

"I want a lot of money!" said a man in his early thirties.

Everyone, including the presenter, laughed.

Then the presenter grew serious. "Of course you do. If we are honest about it, money is the number one reason people attend a seminar like this one, but it is not the only reason. These other visions of success work hand in hand with our desire for increased financial stability. I want you to think of your success in these four areas."

A slide flashed on the screen. It contained four quadrants that read as follows in a clockwise order: *finances, family, health,* and *happiness.*

Someone in the room exclaimed, "Isn't that what we all just said?"

The guru laughed appreciatively. "Exactly, and that slide was made up before this session. We talked about wanting more money, more patience with our families, better health to enjoy our lives, and happiness. There you have the areas of success."

I have to confess that at this point I was a little confused. I had thought I was going to learn the secrets to successful selling. That's what *It's Time to Sell* had sounded like to me—learning how to sell more or how to sell better. I flipped through my notes and reread something the presenter had said earlier: "We will touch on some of the outer game principles, but without the inner game you will never achieve your true potential."

So this was going to be only or mostly about the inner game? For a moment I wondered if perhaps I should quit while I was ahead and see if I could get some of my money back to attend a more nuts-and-bolts seminar on tools for selling.

The thought of leaving the seminar early didn't stay with me for long, mainly because the presenter seemed to have a knack for expressing the very thought I was having at any given moment.

"Now that we have learned about the four quadrants of success, you are probably wondering what this has to do with sales. We will get there very soon indeed. Before dinner, in fact! First, we need to look even more closely at the idea of success.

"A lot of people think success is some pie-in-the-sky idea, but if we are going to become successful, we need to throw those high-level, vague ideas of success out the window. Success is really not about having everything that you want."

A mock groan went up from the crowd.

"And there is a reason for that, which may seem abstract at first. But hear me out. The reason is that the world does not stand still. It is in a constant state of advancement. It is impossible for anyone to stand still, because time is moving forward so we are always either growing or dying.

"Now, what would it mean if we could stand still? Well, let's examine the word *apathy*."

The definition of apathy flashed on the screen:

Apathy is a lack of feeling, emotion, interest, or concern.
Suppression of concern, passion, or motivation.

"Standing still brings apathy. Apathy is the exact opposite of desire!" the presenter announced triumphantly. "Therefore, success is not having everything you want, because getting to the point of having everything would mean you were standing still. Instead, you want to get to the point where you are continuously moving forward. As long as we are moving forward in a given quadrant—or in all of them—we are successful . . . even though we have our own natural ups and downs as we go.

"The best definition I have ever heard—and one I would like to suggest that you adopt—is as follows: 'Success is the progressive realization of a worthy ideal.' That was said in the middle of the twentieth century by Earl Nightingale, who some called the Dean of Personal Development. This definition is pretty much a masterpiece. It implies that it is not your final result that makes you a success, but rather your consistent movement toward a goal. It is the journey rather than the destination.

"Why else would Bill Gates, with his $81 billion net worth, choose to remain an advisor to Microsoft and a global philanthropist?

"Why would Richard Branson, with his $5 billion net worth, choose to write books and help start-up entrepreneurs?

"Because people are at their best when they are moving toward something that they desire. These individuals have a burning desire to help people. They have a passion for life. But they also know that people are never happy when they are standing still. It is the anticipation of putting their all into something that makes people happy."

The male member of an elderly couple spoke up from the table next to mine. "Hello, there. Name's Bill. I grew up on a farm in Ontario. I always saw the chickens and pigs standing around . . ."

The presenter had a questioning look on his face, but he let the man continue.

"But the humans never did. And I realized that's because we have something that animals don't. We have a mind, and a mind needs to be moving forward for its owner to feel successful."

The presenter clapped his hands with joy. "Fantastic, Bill! That reminds me of a line from the Pulitzer Prize-winning playwright Archibald MacLeish: 'The only thing about a man that is man is his mind. Everything else you can find in a pig or a horse.' Anybody else?"

The mother who had expressed being underwhelmed by her day-to-day existence raised her hand. "I'm Cathy. I've definitely noticed that my kids are more excited in the weeks and days leading up to Christmas than they are after Christmas or even later on Christmas Day. I think it's because they're inspired more by the images they have in their minds as to what Christmas will be—the gifts, the togetherness, the laughter, the surprises that might lay in store for them—than they are by the achievement of Christmas, so to speak."

I finally had the courage to raise my hand. I made a false start and then cleared my throat. "I have noticed that I am generally more excited in the weeks leading up to a vacation than I am after the vacation is over. I form an image of what the vacation will bring, and it is my anticipation and my family's anticipation that brings the positive feelings: we'll be with friends, see new things, ride on a roller coaster, listen to waves crashing into the beach outside the patio door. I play these images in my mind while we are saving for the vacation or after we have booked the flight. It is the thought of these images that brings the energy and the excitement."

I thought maybe I had gone on too long, and I was glad that I hadn't announced my name to the room, but the presenter put his hand gently on my shoulder.

"Welcome," he said.

Had he sensed that I was only half in my seat and actually thinking about leaving the conference? I couldn't ponder that possibility for very long, because the presenter was now actually talking about sales!

". . . and so a salesperson is happiest when moving toward a sales target, more so than after the goal has been achieved. It is important to rest and enjoy having achieved a particular goal, but it is more important to set another goal and get moving again. We will set specific goals, but first I wanted you to understand that success in life is growing, success in life is achievement, success in life is making the most of yourself and having a string of goals rather than only one goal."

The youngest participant in the seminar, a young woman who couldn't have been older than twenty-five, raised her hand to ask a question. When she spoke, her words belied a wisdom beyond her years.

"Is this why retirement is a straw man?" she asked. "We think we want to get to a point where we can stop doing all of the things that bring us energy. Why are we even looking for that?"

"Say more," the presenter encouraged her.

"Well, my dad accumulated all of these resources. He worked as the President and CEO of a large marketing company.

He lived to work. When he wasn't working, he was lying on the couch watching TV. Retirement seemed to creep up on him. About four years ago, his company was bought, and he was forced to take a golden parachute. Now, he has a sizable nest egg in the bank but nothing to spend it on. He has been in a downward spiral ever since. I swear, he has aged twenty years in that time."

"That's right," Cathy volunteered. "My father noticed after a couple years of retirement that he was slowing down. So he went and got himself a part-time job. He now works fifteen hours a week as a starter at the local golf course. He gets to meet people and use his social skills. Then, when he wants to take a break, he and my mom head off in their RV exploring areas of the country they didn't know existed. The spring is back in his step."

The presenter nodded his head vigorously. "When we get older we might want to slow down. We might not want to engage in the same level of business activity. But the data shows that when someone retires and does not replace work with something meaningful that can have seriously adverse consequences. And this is because we put all of our eggs into one basket."

He pressed a button, and the slide showing the four quadrants (finances, family, health, and happiness) reappeared on the screen.

"Our definition of success is usually centered on our career, our work, and it includes very little of the other elements, such as our family, our hobbies, and passions, the things that keep us healthy in body, mind, and spirit. In all of these areas, we have to keep moving, keep thriving. Because, let me remind you once more, success is the progressive realization of a worthy ideal. We never arrive at a point when we can cease activity.

"So, now that we know what success is, let's do a little written exercise." At this, the presenter paused, and we picked up our pens in anticipation.

"I want you to think for a moment: Now that we know what success is, what is success *not*? Or, to put it another way, what did you used to think success was? I'll give you a minute to jot down your answers."

I doodled in the margins of the notepad in front of me until I finally scribbled, "Whoever dies with the most toys wins." As it turned out, I wasn't far off from the majority of the participants' answers to the question.

The presenter asked again, "So? What did we used to think defined success?"

"How many people are at your funeral."

"How much money you have in the bank."

"Never having to work again!"

The answers continued in a similar fashion, and I was amazed at how quickly today's events had shifted my mindset. Far from considering success a static thing that could be achieved (or not) once and for all, I now found my mind flooded with things I wanted to accomplish a little bit more of, and then a little bit more after that. It was liberating not having to consider success as occurring at the top of the mountain but rather as ongoing during the incremental parts of the journey. As it turned out, there were a lot of areas of my life that I could imagine improving steadily.

"To conclude our session about success, I want you to bring to mind a question you have probably heard before: Where do you want to be in five years? In some versions of this question, it is three years, but I prefer five years. In the span of five years, you have all the time you need to accomplish anything you set your mind to. But at the same time, it isn't so far away that you can slack—" This brought some laughter from the crowd. "Excuse me, that you can be *apathetic* about it, to borrow a word from our earlier discussion.

"Later in this seminar we will be writing down a very specific vision, because writing down goals does something to the subconscious mind. When written down, the image of your goal becomes firmly planted in your mind, and your actions move you in the direction of achieving it. Some of the changes may be subtle. Others may be more dramatic. But in order to get there, we need specifics. And in order to get specifics, we first need to dream about our successes.

"For your *finances*, what would your life be like if you had a steady stream of passive income coming into your bank account?

"For your *family*, what would life be like if you had value-based relationships with your spouse or partner, your children, your parents, and your extended circle of relations and friends?

"For your *health*, what would life be like if you had the physical body you desire? How would improving your health help you get into a proper flow of everything else you want to achieve?

"For your *happiness*, what would life be like if you were consistently happy, waking up each day ready to conquer something new and really stretch yourself?"

I barely had a chance to contemplate each of these quadrants before my ears perked up at his next set of questions.

"For your *sales*, what would life be like if you had a knack for building genuine relationships with the people you meet, and they automatically trusted you? Imagine the referral network that would come from that!

"I realize full well that some of you are already achieving some degree of success in some of these quadrants, but imagine if you were moving forward in a positive direction in *all* of these areas. Imagine how juicy and fulfilling life would be.

"You *can* achieve success in all of these areas. You can attract the lifestyle that you desire, including the income, relationships, physical condition, and joyful satisfaction that comes from purposeful work in a given direction, provided . . ."

Here the presenter stopped for an unknown reason.

"Provided we don't think we are going to be an overnight success?" a woman at one of the tables in the front volunteered.

The presenter chuckled. "Yes, that too. Achieving success is going to take a lot of hard work. Don't trust anyone who tells you that setting and meeting goals doesn't always take just a little bit longer than you want it to. It's almost as if we have to develop enough to be able to handle the achievement, to change in order to meet the goal. But no, that's not what I was going to say.

"What I was going to say is that success can only come when you stop focusing on your success in a tension-filled way. No longer do I want you to say, 'I'm not achieving my success.' Now I want you to ask, 'How do I achieve my success?' To get up every morning and ask, 'How can I be more successful?'

It all comes when you stop trying too hard. And that begins with gratitude, which we will discuss after our break."

Chapter 3 Summary and Reflective Questions: Success

Success is not about having everything that you want.

The world is in a constant state of advancement. It is impossible for anyone to stand still, because time is moving forward so we are always either growing or dying.

Success is the progressive realization of a worthy ideal.

What do you consider success?

Where do you want to be in three and/or five years in the following areas: finances, family, health, happiness, and sales?

Gratitude

I needed this break even more than I'd needed the previous one. I felt a certain resistance rising again, and I didn't know why. Was I being asked to change my perspective? Did I want to hold on to some outmoded ways of doing things? Could I ever decisively win this battle? I took a long walk outside the conference facility and tried to straighten out my mind to be as receptive as I possibly could. When I returned to the door of our meeting room, I pushed it open and took a deep breath.

The presenter had switched to a slide that contained a single word:

Gratitude

When everyone had returned to the room, the presenter resumed. "As you now know, a successful life is a composition of successful days. And the number one ingredient that I have found that helps set up a successful day is gratitude.

"We hear a lot about gratitude, but what is it, really? Gratitude is an attitude that sets off a chain reaction of positive energy. You can only take from the world what you put into it.

"Remember our quadrants: finances, family, health, and happiness . . . and let's add sales in there as well. These are the areas for us to begin being grateful for.

"Now, you may be saying to yourself. How can I be grateful for my finances if I have not saved enough, or if I get to the end of the week and I owe more in bills than I get in my paycheck? Or how can I be grateful for my sales figures when my boss says they are not enough?

"Well, let me ask you. Last week, did your company pay you an average or an above average wage?"

The young man in his early thirties, who earlier in the afternoon had volunteered his desire for a lot of money, grudgingly answered, "Above average."

"So, that is something to be grateful for, isn't it? Now, you may be saying to yourself, 'But I owe so much on my mortgage that I am only paying the monthly interest.'

How did he know the exact financial situation Nora and I were in? I wondered.

"But did you wake up this morning in Fargo?"

I found myself shouting out, "Yes, and I came five thousand miles to get here!"

"Well, there you go," the presenter said, as he chuckled a bit. "You should be grateful for that. I know I am.

"We all have conflict and stress in our lives." The presenter stopped by Cathy's table on his walk around the room. "You may be saying to yourself, 'I had an argument with my son last night about him not doing his homework when I asked him to.' But who is the most important person in your son's world right now? *You.* He may not say it, but you know deep down that you are. The bond between a parent and a child, while it may not express itself every moment of every day, is something to be grateful for.

"So, folks, do you notice your energy level changing as we go through these examples?"

Heads around the room were nodding in the affirmative.

"Can somebody share an example?"

A middle-aged woman raised her hand. "Hi, I'm Alyse. Yesterday I went on a four-mile run. I'm not in great shape, and I had to walk twice, but I did find myself thinking, 'Well Alyse, at least you're completely healthy. You don't have a disease. You don't have a broken bone or a twisted muscle. You don't even have any kind of flu.' "

"And did you realize all of that in the moment?" the presenter asked. When the woman nodded, he continued, "And what effect did that have on you?"

"Well, it allowed me to straighten my posture. I was able to enjoy the day more, almost as if a burden had been released."

The presenter replied, "Imagine starting off your day or taking a moment during your day to practice gratitude. Because gratitude is the place to start when you are creating a positive vision of your future. Gratitude helps you change the thoughts of 'I can't do this. I can't have this. I can't be this,' because gratitude says, 'Well, you did that. You got that. And you became that.'

"Remember, success is about being in process, about moving forward. There are a lot of things to be grateful for right now. If I were to ask you to list five things—"

The somewhat self-important man in his thirties surprised the room when he interrupted the presenter with his next contribution: "I've been a little bit hit or miss on the practice of writing down the five things I'm grateful for every morning, although I have done it in the past for periods of time . . . and I do know that when I'm consistently doing that, my days start off in a highly aware state, like I'm getting into the day on a very positive footing."

"Exactly," the presenter declared. "And your name, sir?"

"John," the hotshot said.

"John, what you just said jibes wonderfully with the whole concept that the universe will not enhance your life until you are grateful for what you currently have. Now, let's take it one step further.

"I am going to suggest something that you may think is completely out there. I don't want to get too metaphysical here, but it has been proven, time and time again, that the practice of gratitude sets things in motion so that you will attract to yourself what you desire.

"Now, what if you practice gratitude for things you desire in your life that you do not yet have?"

Someone in the room let out a low whistle, like that idea was really hitting home. I confess that I was still struggling to feel gratitude for what I presently had, so I was relieved when the presenter concluded the day's session by assigning us the homework of getting in touch with twenty-five things for which we were currently grateful.

When I left the meeting room for the day, my head was spinning. Fortunately, I had my gratitude list homework to focus on. I kept it with me while I ate dinner in town and while I relaxed in my hotel room afterward. At first the items on my list seemed hard to come up with and, truth be told, made me feel a little ashamed of myself. I was grateful for my family—they were the ones standing by me even though I hadn't been very present for them lately. I was grateful for my wife, who still wanted me to go to Fargo even though we had hardly any money in the bank.

But gradually these thoughts brightened when I realized everything I had been gifted with: two healthy children, my education, the natural beauty of the area where I lived, lively conversation with my friends, the ability to live in a country that allowed me entrepreneurial mobility, the state-of-the-art gym I belonged to (even if I did go there only occasionally), the tools and skills I had accumulated thus far in my woodworking hobby, a beautiful office that was conducive to long periods of high quality work, and so on.

By the time I turned off the light, my gratitude list was well past twenty-five things and on its way to fifty or more. And the despair I had felt while driving to Fargo seemed like a very distant memory indeed.

Chapter 4 Summary and Reflective Questions: Gratitude

Gratitude is an attitude that sets off a chain reaction of positive energy. You can only take from the world what you put into it.

Gratitude helps you change the thoughts of "I can't do this. I can't have this. I can't be this," because gratitude says, "Well, you did that. You got that. And you became that."

What are five things for which you are currently grateful in each of the following areas: finances, family, health, happiness, and sales?

Day Two: AM

Attitude

I didn't sleep well that night. It wasn't that I slept badly—it was just that I woke up every two hours with another bunch of things to add to my gratitude list. I thought of our great neighbors, a retired couple who were always kind to our two children and kept an eye on things whenever we went away for a weekend. I thought of my access to clean water and healthy food (not that I always made the healthiest eating choices, but I could because I had the opportunity). I thought of my clients who it seemed had stuck with me even when I was wrapped up in my own worries and negativity. I thought of people who had forgiven me in the past, of how far our society had come technologically, of that inner voice that gave me good ideas, of all the travels I had come through safely. The list went on and on.

We had been given a workbook for the seminar, and I had carefully placed it by my nightstand so that I could read some of it before bed and when I woke up, but my gratitude list had simply taken over all of my activities, and I thought our presenter would appreciate that. It was as if this list were laying some important groundwork for the day ahead, and I could feel its effect on me. That effect was hard to describe: a floating, unbothered kind of feeling, a resilience that would enable me to respond with patience to anything that didn't go my way, and an expectation that some things, the right things, would go my way.

At breakfast in the hotel I still had my gratitude list with me. It was up to eighty-seven things even though we had only been asked to record twenty-five. I felt more peaceful than I did on an average morning, when I would bolster myself with two cups of coffee in order to meet what felt like a backbreaking burden of debt. With this feeling of relative lightness, I witnessed a commonplace scene that, at the time, struck me as amazing.

A man who was in the buffet line with me was arguing with one of the line cooks who was stocking the breakfast items.

"Can't anyone around here make an omelet? This is literally the third time I've had to come back here. First, it was because the dish had ham in it, and the second time was because the middle wasn't cooked all the way through. You've got a goddamned omelet maker! Didn't anybody stop and read the directions?"

The situation would have been a lot for any morning, but today I watched the events unfold with especially wide eyes. The argumentative man probably had a long day ahead of him; perhaps he was under pressure from his boss, like I was. But he was alienating himself so utterly from the world around him.

Even I could see that, and I normally don't pay much attention to other people's business.

As I looked around for someone with whom to share my newfound insight, I saw our presenter standing near the back of the line for breakfast. He gave me a knowing glance and mouthed the word "att–i–tude." I nodded slowly, not wanting to draw more attention to the scene, but I got the message.

When I arrived at the meeting room, the presenter was waiting for me at the door. I hadn't seen where he had disappeared with his breakfast. I'd just thought he had material to prepare for the day and had taken the meal back to his room.

"What is your name?" he asked me.

"I'm Colin."

"Great to meet you, Colin. Say, could I ask you a favor? Could you lead off today's session with a description of what we witnessed at breakfast?"

At first, I didn't know how to react. I didn't want to say no to him, but I didn't really view myself as an accomplished public speaker. I didn't feel confident in my ability to deliver the story the way that I imagined he wanted it told.

Then I heard a curious idea in my head: *To get the energy to do the thing, you just have to do the thing.*

I think I understood the message. I had witnessed the guy's bad attitude. Telling the story should be easy to do if I framed it the right way in my mind.

I found myself agreeing to the presenter's request. When he gave me the signal, I started telling the story any way I could think of, and after four or five words it was amazing—I truly was off to the races!

I didn't know where all the details were coming from, but I described the scene so vividly: facial expressions, gestures, tones of voice. It was as if I were having some kind of breakthrough. I had found the energy to do the thing by just doing the thing.

When I finished, the presenter took the microphone from me. "Thank you, Colin. Excellent work! What Colin has just described are the results of attitude."

The word appeared on the screen.

"What is an attitude? An attitude is a way of thinking or feeling, about someone or something, that is reflected in our behavior. As the composite of our thoughts and feelings, our attitude determines our actions, which are then reflected in our results."

The screen showed this chain reaction:

"Are you with me? Our attitudes determine our actions in the presence of others and are then reflected back to us in the form of people's attitudes toward us. We cannot receive what we do not give. The world in which we live is governed by a number of natural laws, and one of those laws—perhaps the most important, because it pertains to the results in our lives—is the Law of Cause and Effect.

"This law dictates that the results we experience in our lives align very well with the energy and contribution we put out. We get what we expect. And that means that—and this has been proven—the main determinant of success in our lives is attitude.

"Now, I know what you're thinking." The presenter paused in his walk around the room and stood next to a table near the front. Most of the attendees had unconsciously chosen the same seats as the previous day, perhaps in a holdover from the grade school days of assigned seating.

"Or maybe you're not thinking anything yet . . . maybe it's too early! On some level we all think that our attitudes are beyond our control. We focus on how we have had it tough. Maybe we come from less fertile backgrounds and have had less privilege, which we think means that we face a tougher battle.

"But I want to say to you that, each morning, we all wake up in the same place. We can either say that the past is the past, use it to our advantage, and look forward . . . or we can be buried under it. We each face that decision every day when we get up and start over. We establish our attitudes each morning when we wake up.

"So, what was your attitude when you woke up this morning?"

One of the women at the table next to the presenter spoke up. "I don't think I had one. I mean, how would I know?"

The presenter laughed. "Well, did you make an ugly scene at breakfast like the man Colin and I witnessed?"

"No," she said, "I didn't have breakfast."

"Oh, you should eat breakfast! But, seriously, in our worlds the results we get are reflections of our attitudes, in perfect correlation: good attitude, good results; fair or average attitude, fair or average results; bad attitude, undercooked eggs with ham—bad results.

"An easy way to determine your attitude is to answer the question, 'How do people react to you when you greet them?' Are they smiling? Are they cheerful? The answer is very likely a reflection of your attitude.

"So, what does this have to do with sales? Well, would you agree that, for the most part, anything we want in life must come to us with and through other people?"

The room murmured in assent.

"If you are in sales, your income relies on people buying and using your product or service, in the same way that owners of a company rely on the work of their employees. Or, if you are a parent, how you feel on a daily basis can be determined by how your children are acting toward you. We need people in our lives, and we need positive relationships with these people in order to move our lives forward. The quality of each of these relationships is determined by our attitudes toward ourselves and our relationships, because people react to our attitudes."

The presenter switched to a slide that contained a quotation:

"Human beings, by changing the inner attitudes of their minds, can change the outer aspects of their lives." —William James

After we had pondered that quote for a couple minutes, the presenter set us to examining our attitudes about the four quadrants we had been discussing: health, finances, family, and happiness. At first, I was a little stuck. I mean, how do you uncover your attitudes about these areas of life? As we were brainstorming in our workbooks, the presenter changed the slide so that it showed only one word:

Expectancy

The presenter explained, "In his program entitled *Lead the Field*, Earl Nightingale suggested that the attitudes that bring results are gratitude and expectancy. We've talked about gratitude quite a bit to this point, but what about expectancy? How we act and conduct ourselves in all of our affairs indicates the results we seek. Our habitual way of thinking shows through in this aspect of our attitude.

"So? Time's up. What do you expect in terms of health?"

A man who was wearing clothing that might have been a size too big for him spoke up from the middle of the room. "I'm probably thirty pounds overweight. When I was young I used to eat whenever things felt out of control or I felt like people weren't hearing or seeing me. As I got older I went on diets but I was always like a yo-yo—up twenty pounds, down forty pounds, up thirty pounds. My doctor said that was bad for me, and since I couldn't keep the weight off I just decided I was going to live with my weight the way it was. So I would say my attitude—my expectancy—about my weight has been negative."

"That's good," the presenter said. "I mean, it's not—"

The man laughed, which gave the rest of us permission to have a tension-relieving chuckle as well.

"And, for those people trying to figure things out, how do you know that this is your attitude about your weight?"

"Well, you can just look at my clothes, for one thing. I'm hiding under here. I also realized that I'm avoiding the gym, often taking different routes home so I don't see the gym as I drive by. That kind of poor attitude is getting me poor results, I guess."

One by one the workshop attendees began opening up about how their negative attitudes in various areas of their lives had produced poor results.

John, the crisply dressed younger man who I originally had pegged as a hotshot, revealed the following: "From a young age I began to associate having toys with a feeling of worth. But I am living a lie to the outside world. I have all the toys and the BMW, but little do people know that I am two paychecks away from financial embarrassment."

"So, what is the attitude?"

"The attitude is that I am hanging on by a thread. That I'm a phony, and that any day people are going to find out, which leaves my mind in a constant state of desperation to stay one step ahead of ruin."

Bill, the older man, spoke up next, "Can we say something good, too?"

Encouraged by the presenter's welcoming hand gesture, Bill continued. "Well, I mean, there are areas of my life that are tripping me up, to be sure. But my relationship with my wife isn't in that column. My wife and I met when we were thirteen years old. We were high school sweethearts. Our bond is so deep, like we are on the same wavelength, I think in part because we expect to be."

The man continued, but my mind had gone to my relationship with Nora. It was the same with us. Many times throughout the day I think about texting her just to say hi, and within seconds I receive a text from her that says the same thing—it's like she's reading my mind. We have been through our ups and downs, but I can honestly say that the strength of our relationship comes directly from our attitudes toward each other.

"Okay, one more—the hardest one: happiness. Anybody?"

Alyse, the woman who looked to be in her early fifties and was just getting back into exercise, described how she had jumped around quite a bit vocationally. She was now looking to be a business coach. About five years ago she had moved from Seattle, Washington, to the much smaller town of Liberty Lake at the other end of the state. Liberty Lake is a close-knit town with a population of only about 7,500. After a few questions from the presenter, Alyse opened up that she did not feel as though she had been accepted by the people of Liberty Lake.

"Have you made an effort to get out to meet people? And perhaps invite the people you meet to join you on your runs . . . or just to come over for tea?"

"I love tea! But no, I haven't. I think that's the realization I'm coming to—the town is giving me back a reflection of my attitude."

"Well, so now we know that we need to consciously choose what our attitudes will be and practice them daily until they become habit. After the break, we'll discuss the source of our attitudes some more and really get down to the root of the problem.

"But for now, let's just focus on this fact: Most people do not decide what their attitudes will be. Most people simply react to the various stimuli that they encounter throughout the day. A person cuts you off while driving, you let that change your mood. You get an email indicating that your coworker has called in sick, you let that dictate your mood for the rest of the day. You fall off the wagon after a few days of healthy eating, you decide you are going back to your old way of eating. You shout at your child because he has not come home on time, and then you walk around the house all evening grumpy.

"Your reactions are habits, but they can be changed through practice. Now, think about this in relation to sales. What is your attitude toward the customer?"

He advanced the presentation to the next slide:

Are you pushing, or are you pulling?

"I have a confession to make. I *hate* being sold. Yes, you heard that right. A guy who hangs his hat on the sales profession hates being sold.

"The minute I feel the push, I start to shut down. I will even turn down a salesperson who is selling me something I really need if I feel the push. I will avoid certain situations at all cost to avoid feeling like I am being sold.

"What does 'being sold' mean? The best way I can describe it is to show it. Colin, can you come back up here for a minute?"

My fear of public speaking was really getting a workout today! Fortunately, I didn't have to say much in this demonstration. The presenter just asked me to stand at attention with my arms at my sides. He stood in front of me with his hands stretched out toward me, leaving about three inches between his hands and my body.

"Colin is the prospect, and I am the seller. Now, as the seller, I have a product or service that I want to sell to him. 'Sir, I have this bright and shiny X that will deliver Y result for you.' What do you say?"

"Well, that depends. Do I see something I desire in the product or service?"

"Yes, but you are not quite ready to make the purchase. I realize this, so I take a slightly different angle in an attempt to bridge the gap between us. I get closer,"—here about half of the three inches between us disappeared—"and I whisper, 'Look at Alyse. She bought X last year, and look at her Y now!' Now what do you want to do?"

I instinctively backed up, restoring not only the original three inches between us, but adding another six inches for good measure.

"Exactly! That is what the push approach does. It pushes the customer away. You may be asking, 'Okay, then, sales guru, how do you recommend I sell my product?' A mentor of mine advised me early in my career to kiss the girl who leans toward you. I thought it was brilliant at the time and have used it as an analogy in describing my approach to sales ever since. I would like to suggest that the best sales approach is to sell your product or service to the customer who is leaning toward you. I call this a pull strategy. Your job as a sales professional is to pull rather than push.

"How do you bridge the gap in a pull strategy? You educate, and you inspire."

The presenter returned his outstretched hands to three inches away from me, and then he started slowly pulling his hands back to his body.

"Colin isn't ready to buy right now. I understand that, yet I keep looking forward. I keep track of my own attitude and do not bring one iota of tension into the sales process by pushing. Instead, I educate potential customers, directly when asked and indirectly through social networks where I share the latest and greatest about my industry and, on occasion, about my product or service. When Colin, or anyone else, asks about my offerings, I provide them with the answers. I inspire by using my product or service myself and being a demonstration of its results.

"So, what do you think? As a sales professional, do you push with an attitude of need or do you pull with an attitude of expectancy?

"Let's think about that while we take a break."

Chapter 5 Summary and Reflective Questions: Attitude

An attitude is a way of thinking or feeling, about someone or something, that is reflected in our behavior.

The law of cause and effect dictates that the results we experience in our lives align very well with the energy and contribution we put out. We get what we expect. And that means that the main determinant of success in our lives is attitude.

What was your attitude when you woke up this morning?

How do people react to you when you greet them?

As a sales professional, do you push with an attitude of need or do you pull with an attitude of expectancy?

Paradigms

"Okay, are we ready? Everybody get their cup of coffee or five-hour energy, or whatever. . . ."

The presenter wandered by one of the tables and picked up an attendee's sixteen-ounce energy drink. "Wow," he read, "JAVA MONSTER. It's that intense, huh?"

Amidst laughter, he continued, "Well, you know what? It is that intense. We're talking about attitudes and habits in certain areas of our lives. The stakes are enormous."

A picture of a circus elephant flashed on the screen in front of us.

"I'm going to tell you a story that's not that pretty right now. It's about elephants. Now, we connect with elephants. Like us, they cry and play. They mourn their dead and treasure their young. Unlike us, though, they cannot break down a paradigm.

"What is a paradigm? A paradigm is a collection of habits in a particular area of our lives.

"These elephants are five tons in weight and three meters high. Oh, I forgot I was in the U.S.! Let's see, they are about ten feet tall and weigh about ten thousand pounds. And those aren't the only staggering statistics: an elephant has over forty thousand muscles in its trunk alone. Elephants in captivity, like these we are seeing on the screen, even though they are held by chains, they could break free with ease. But why don't they?

"It's called conditioning. Or, to put it another way, they don't know what they don't know. Captured when young, chained to a stake, they try desperately to break free, but at that size they are not strong enough. Eventually, they stop trying. The paradigm has been set, and thereafter, they are doomed to a life in chains, acting unlike their true nature. Some have even died in fires when they were chained to stakes they could have easily escaped from.

"Now, this is awful. And, personally, I don't go to the circus. But how does this elephant analogy apply to you and your life? What were you indirectly—or perhaps even directly—told at a young age that you could not achieve in this world? Because those are your paradigms.

"But remember, there is a very big difference between you and an elephant. You can change your paradigms. You can take an idea and turn it into something magnificent.

"Have you ever observed successful, well-balanced people and wondered what their key to success is? What their driving force is? Why they don't seem to *react* to their environment? Instead, they *respond*. The reason is that they are in charge of their paradigms.

"You see, at a very young age we decide who we are and what we can accomplish. We take input from other people—sometimes our friends and neighbors, definitely our parents—and we combine that with our own creative interpretations of events, and our paradigms are set. Notice that I said, creative *interpretations* of events, not the events themselves. Our minds take in all of the stimuli from our past experiences—the touch, the sight, the taste, the smell, the sounds—and we add to that our creative interpretations, and voila . . . we have *you!*

"Is this clear to everybody? Does anybody want to volunteer a paradigm of theirs that was created by their creative interpretation of an event?"

The presenter was walking around again, and I had a sinking feeling as he approached our table. He placed his hand gently on my shoulder.

"Colin, I promise, if you give us one of your paradigms right now, I will leave you alone for the rest of the weekend."

I couldn't help but laugh. He was so skilled at putting people at ease.

"Well, I don't know if this is what you want," I started, "but this is what I was thinking. . . ."

I saw the presenter's wordless, encouraging smile, and I took a deep breath.

"Okay, I hate baseball. That's my paradigm. But listen, here's why. When I was in fifth grade, we moved to a new town. I think I must have been eleven years old, and my mother decided to enroll me in baseball. Now, I'd never played baseball in my life, except throwing the ball back and forth with my dad and maybe playing a bit of street baseball. I never knew the rules of the game.

"So, the first time I was up at bat, I hit the ball and ran to first base. I stood there. So far, so good! Then the next batter came up, and I decide I'm going to steal—hey, I wanted to impress the other kids, right?—so I ran to second base. No coach told me to run. I did it on my own instinct.

"But what I didn't realize was that my friend Greg, we used to call him Zonk because he was a great big fella, he was already on second! So now he had to run to third or we would both be out, and when he slid into third he broke his leg. I never played a game of baseball after that. At eleven years old, that experience, plus what I guess you would call my creative interpretation, created such a negative image of baseball in my mind—"

"Exactly!" the presenter cried out. "Exactly. Hey, Colin, thanks for sharing. And I'm sure it's okay that you said you hate baseball. They probably don't play a lot of baseball up here anyway, right? Now, if you'd said you hate hockey here in North Dakota, you might be in trouble.

"What Colin has just shown us—and no offense to you, my friend—is an example of the Average Cycle. The present results, a friend's broken leg, form the overriding paradigm when it comes to Colin and baseball."

On the screen flashed a flowchart:

"The results were that Colin's friend broke his leg. This created the paradigm that baseball was bad, which influenced

Colin's feelings about hating baseball. As far as his actions, well, I'm sure Colin doesn't head out to the old ballpark and grab some peanuts and Cracker Jack and root, root, root for the home team. Am I right, Colin?"

I nodded my head vigorously in agreement.

"Now, obviously, it's not just Colin. Most of us are influenced by our present results. Those results determine our thoughts. Our thoughts, in turn, control our feelings, which produce our actions, and thus our continued results.

"It's a cycle. Average individuals, who have not consciously made a decision to change their results, focus on their current results, which create their paradigms and their feelings, which eventually produce the same results over and over again.

"We want to break this Average Cycle. We're not going to go into the psychological depth here of how each of your paradigms was created by a mixture of other people's input and your own creative interpretations of events and becomes our negative self-talk. But we are certainly going to look closely at our paradigms to find those that serve us so that we can use them to our advantage. Our other job is to find those that do not serve us and change them.

A new flowchart flashed on the screen:

The Cycle of the Successful

"Successful people are not controlled by their paradigms. Instead, they form a very clear picture of a worthy ideal or vision of what they want to achieve. That image brings with it feelings of positive emotion and energy, otherwise known as self-motivation, that in turn produce actions that attract the necessary growth and progress into their lives in the form of results.

"How do you get rid of dark in a room? You turn on the light. How do you get rid of the cold? You turn on the heat, or you build a fire. When you build a fire, the cold is gone. In a similar way, if we want confidence, we need to get rid of the paradigm of insecurity. If we want wealth, we need to get rid of the paradigm of poverty.

"We need to focus on what we want."

I felt a little as if I were having an out-of-body experience. How many times had I heard something similar to what was being presented today? I had read books and listened to audio recordings, but I hadn't experienced this sudden emotional impact of realizing how this stuff applied to my past and how it could be applied positively to my future.

In a flash I understood that I was the sum total of all my thoughts up to this point in life. It had been a rough period of months stretching into a few years, but that was only the result of my having talked myself into a paradigm in which I was limited, at best, and a failure, at worst.

I finally saw my present results as only the tip of the iceberg. The events that were occurring in my environment were still there, but the bigger reality, by far, lay submerged under the ocean in the form of my negative self-talk and my creative interpretations of experiences, which might very well be wrong. My paradigms had created the foundation of my being in a very difficult spot. And it was those paradigms that I absolutely had to learn more about.

During the rest of the morning session, the presenter asked us a series of reflective questions designed to root out the paradigms that were controlling our every move. We frantically scribbled our responses as one slide after another deeply probed our current attitudes.

Finances: What do your current results tell you about your paradigms about money?

- *How much do you earn?*
- *Do you save a portion of your income?*
- *Do you spend every cent before it is earned?*
- *Do you give to people in need?*

While considering this slide, I realized that my financial situation was important to me. It was where the rubber met the road, in other words. If I didn't have that in place, I couldn't really focus on other things in my life. That didn't seem like a disempowering paradigm; it felt more neutral. What I found troubling, however, was my deep-rooted belief that material wealth was a sign to others about my worth. Therefore, in an effort to make people like me, I regularly spent more than I earned.

Family: What do your current results tell you about your paradigms about family?

- *How are your relationships with your parents and siblings?*
- *How is your relationship with your spouse or significant other?*

- *How are your relationships with your children? With your closest friends?*

The results of my paradigm exploration in the family quadrant were a little more positive than in the finances quadrant. I recalled how Nora and I had been childhood sweethearts. All along, we had planned to get married early in life—we loved each other and wanted to start a family to share our joy with our children's grandparents while they were still young.

Together we have some wonderfully deep friendships, and our families get together as one big family for special occasions. I think there are a number of ways to define family, but however you define it, family is necessary for a complete life. Having everything I want but being alone would not be satisfying. I need others with whom to share prosperity.

Health: What do your current results tell you about your paradigms about health?

- *Are you at your ideal weight?*
- *How is your energy level?*
- *Why do you eat (examples: for nourishment, to fill a void, because you were told you need your three square meals a day or to finish everything on your plate)?*
- *Do you exercise?*
- *What do you do when you feel your belt getting a little tighter?*

I had to admit that I felt better about myself when I was lean and mean. Not only did I think more clearly then—perhaps from having more oxygen in my blood—but a positive physical self-image seemed to cause a reservoir of energy to pour into all of the other aspects of my life. My current results were, frankly, a little flabbier and more lethargic than I desired, and yet I realized they were the direct result of my paradigms, of how I felt about myself.

Happiness: What do your current results tell you about your paradigms about happiness?

- *Do you choose to be happy?*
- *Are you grateful?*
- *How do you react when someone tells you no? Or when you encounter a setback or obstacle? Do you get mad, or do you just move on?*

This was a tough one. Was it true that I wasn't a very happy person right now? My patience level was certainly low. I did find myself, if not obsessed with bad things happening, at least expecting more bad than good in my life. This category was probably the most brutal reality check, but I knew from other times in my life that when you find the strength to face the worst parts of your reality they almost immediately seem to improve a bit, to shift to an upswing.

Sales: What do your current results tell you about your paradigms about the sales profession?

- *Do you believe that sales is a worthy profession?*
- *Do you believe that sales is a numbers game?*

- *Do you believe that relationships are important to sales?*
- *Do you believe that salespeople are responsible for helping their customers solve problems?*
- *Has your commission check hovered around the same amount for the past few years?*

I was completely unprepared for my responses to these questions. It was like the baseball story. Before I knew it, my mind was filled with images of used car salesmen and men who sold knives and encyclopedias door-to-door in my childhood neighborhood. Those guys knew how to push, as opposed to the pull approach we had learned earlier this morning.

And me? My paradigm, which was clear to me now, was that I viewed sales as an unworthy profession. After all these years of being in sales myself!

Fortunately, I didn't have time to obsess about this discovery, because the other attendees seemed to echo my internal reactions.

One man at my table, who looked to be about my age, spoke up shyly. "I'm Perry, and this is the first time I've said anything in this workshop, because I didn't really feel like I had anything to say. But it just hit me. You know, my father was a lawyer, and his father was a lawyer. And I was raised to believe that I needed to be in a profession, whether as a lawyer, or a doctor, or an engineer. Now, there is a crucial sales function to my business, but for a long time, right up to today, really, I viewed that as an irritant or beneath me. It's so silly, though, that paradigm! I mean, in law firms the most prized lawyers are the ones who bring in business—they call them rainmakers—and what is that? That's just sales."

"You are a brave man, Perry," the presenter said.

A brave man, indeed. We all needed to dig deeper into our paradigms in each of these four quadrants and in sales.

"The answers to these questions paint pictures of the paradigms that control our behaviors," the presenter advised us. "To change our results we must change our paradigms and then integrate those new beliefs with our behaviors. For now, however, we are simply challenging our current beliefs.

"Do you *believe* that you can multiply your income by using the right approach to sales? Do you *believe* that you can reach your ideal body weight if you eat right and exercise consistently over a period of time? Do you *believe* that if you show gratitude toward your family members that they will feel more love from you and therefore return it?

"If we want to get serious about building new paradigms, we will need to make mental shifts. Perry, for example, will need to realize the critical nature of sales and how nothing moves in this world unless someone buys it and someone sells it. To buy something we need to be educated about it. Sales is really just the art of finding out if what we are offering is in line with what the other person needs.

"A lot of people buy stuff they don't need, but that's not what I'm talking about. If you're not selling something that people really need or you're not working at a company that supports you, you're at the wrong company. You need to offer a product that you are passionate about and that you believe in.

"After that, you need to have the right sales paradigm in place, where sales is viewed as an equal exchange of energy and simply a formalization of an existing, functional relationship. We need to make a decision to change our paradigms, and we do this one habit at a time.

"And for those of you who are focused on the health quadrant, you can probably start by changing some of your habits at lunch!"

Chapter 6 Summary and Reflective Questions: Paradigms

A paradigm is a collection of habits in a particular area of our lives.

Successful people are not controlled by their paradigms.

What do your current results tell you about your paradigms about money, family, health, happiness, and sales?

DAY TWO: PM

Setting the X

Lunch was an unusual experience for me that day. I can't recall ever before having been so conscious of my choices. I'm sure it wasn't the first time I had selected cottage cheese, fruit, yogurt, and a large bottle of water. But I don't recall any previous time *knowing* that choosing the hamburger, fries, and diet Coke (my traditional meal of champions) would be a direct result of the paradigm in which I had given up on my aspirations to feel fit and trim. For me, the hamburger meal choice reflected my unhappiness and my hope that the food would cheer me up.

This would be a lot to consider at every meal time or during every minute of the day! When I returned to the meeting room, I honestly didn't know how much I had left in the tank for the rest of the day. My mind felt full to the brim, and the fact that we hadn't yet reached the summit left me, frankly, a little breathless.

The presenter seemed to understand this might be the case for many of us, because the meeting room was filled with music, an unobtrusive yet groovy jazz that enabled me to take a few deep breaths. When the next session of the workshop started, the presenter asked us to hearken back to the beginning of the entire seminar in order to help ground ourselves.

"Remember that you are here because you have a desire. It was that desire to be, do, or have more in life that brought you to this seminar."

This much was true. I could always connect with my yearning to achieve the goals that I saw in my mind's eye. The fact that I hadn't quite pulled off these goals was what weighed heavily on me most of the time. But if all I had to do was focus on my desire, well, I could do that.

The presenter continued, "The next step we are going to take is to imagine your life in its ideal condition. Putting together that vision is of critical importance, because that vision will inspire you to live your life in a way that supports the vision. We will then focus on substituting your new vision for the vision you presently have, the one that is not giving you the results you desire.

"We all have a vision. Is yours a negative one? Do you focus on what you are not getting out of life? Or do you have a positive vision, one in which you are constantly growing and working toward what you want to do, be, and have—toward that successive realization of a worthy ideal?"

I started feeling badly, thinking that by now I should probably be converted or something, and have a positive vision, yet as I reflected I saw that I was still struggling with negative self-talk and a tendency to expect or fear the worst, which was why the presenter's next statements put me more at ease.

"The majority of people are negatively focused. They have a set of paradigms around each of these areas of life, and an associated set of habits, which are the cause of the negative results they're getting. It's very simple: The universe responds to our thoughts as they are embodied in our feelings, first, and in our actions, later.

"Once we recognize, however, that everyone has a vision, whether positive or negative, and once we do the analysis around what our existing paradigms are, then we can pursue a positive vision in which anything can be changed by changing what we focus on.

"It is really that straightforward: By continuing to focus on current results and allowing those results to dictate our thoughts, feelings, and actions, we will continue to get the same results. If, however, we realize—fully and completely—that we are the product of a habitual way of thinking that forms our paradigms in all the important areas of our lives, then we can write a new script."

The presenter changed the slide:

Vision Creation Process

"Self-motivation is the key to achieving success in life. Self-motivation pours forth when you have a compelling vision in your mind of the life that you would like to lead.

"Can we pause for a moment, so I can tell you a personal story?"

The exhales in the room seemed to indicate that we were all ready to hear an example from the presenter. Just as I was glad that he hadn't tried to bowl us over with his fabulous successes at the beginning of the seminar, I was now ready to follow someone else's example for a few moments and give the relentless self-examination a rest. I hoped that the presenter's story would show not only how he had "arrived" but also some of the struggles he had gone through to get there. And I was not disappointed.

"I would like to tell you about the power of the vision creation process. In doing so, I will be speaking intimately about income, but I don't want you to interpret this as ego. This is just an example of how it works, of how it can work for all of us.

"I started my career working in marketing. My starting salary was $43,000 per year. That's not much, right? But I thought that's all I could get. My mom had always told me when I was growing up that a career that paid $50,000 was a really good living. A year into my career I started a home-based business as a means of earning more income. Through brute force I earned an additional $30,000 that first year. However, although I had temporary motivation, I hadn't changed my expectations, my paradigm of what making a good living looked like. The next year my income from the sideline business decreased to exactly $7,000, bringing my annual income to a total of $50,000. I got exactly what I expected in my vision.

"After reading Napoleon Hill's book *Think and Grow Rich*, I decided to form the vision of growing my income to $225,000. This was a consciously chosen number based on the lifestyle I wanted. I decided that the best way for me to reach this number was to use my skills, values, and purpose—which you will hear more about—to be of service in the sales profession.

I made the move to this industry, and within twelve months I was making my desired income.

"I then set my vision even higher, and I am now making many multiples more. Again, I tell you this only to inspire. Has anyone else had an experience similar to what I am describing?"

An attractive woman who had always chosen to sit along the wall on the opposite side of the room from me raised her hand for the first time in the seminar.

"When I was first starting out in sales, I did that. My friend and I called it 'Setting the X.' We each set a number we wanted to make for the year. We didn't tell the numbers to each other, but we wrote them down and tossed the pieces of paper into her non-working fireplace. At the end of the year, we got together for some holiday cheer and unfolded our numbers. I had made the exact amount I had written down, like to the dollar. It was scary!

"What I didn't realize until today," she continued, "is that number is still my number. I haven't changed it in my mind, and I haven't written down a different number since that year, so I guess that is why I just keep making the same amount year after year."

"A perfect example! At first, it may have even seemed absurd to you to name the number that you did, because your present existence didn't include the conditions that seemed to be required to create it, but when you set the vision the conditions came to meet you. And then you got stuck there, because you didn't engage with the vision as a continual, unfolding process.

"This process of vision creation can be applied to more than just our finances, of course. In fact, creating new paradigms needs to happen in all four of the quadrants—health, finances, family, and happiness—plus your relationship to sales. Keep that in mind as we take a very short break, and then come back to craft our new visions."

Chapter 7 Summary and Reflective Questions: Setting the X

We all have a vision.

Is your vision a negative one? Do you focus on what you are not getting out of life?

Is your vision a neutral one? Do you focus on maintaining your existing life?

Or do you have a positive vision, one in which you are constantly growing and working toward what you want to do, be, and have?

A Vision Shift

During the break, I thought about creating new paradigms for myself, about shifting my vision in the five areas the presenter had outlined. Could it happen, just like that? It may seem strange, but the real problem I was having was how to know what would be too much to ask for. I have never thought of myself as having low self-esteem, but I did find myself a bit shy when it came to asking for what I really wanted.

My fog of confusion began to lift when the presenter resumed the discussion.

"Remember, shifting your vision doesn't require a lot of work translating your old paradigms into new ones. There is no science behind changing a paradigm that doesn't serve you; you simply have to replace it with a new one. And it isn't like this is going to happen overnight. It requires sustained focus, beginning with writing out your new vision.

"A worthwhile analogy might be dying cloth. It is not a matter of just throwing the cloth in the dye. You have to soak, dry, soak, and dry many times before the new color becomes dominant. This afternoon we are simply putting the cloth in the dye for the first time. The process will continue tomorrow as we learn techniques for relaxation, visualization, and affirmation, which will help the dye set in deeper and deeper.

"Are you ready?"

The presenter led us through a recap of the five areas in which we would be creating a new vision: health, finances, family, happiness, and our relationship to sales. We were encouraged to flip back through our notes and reread our existing paradigms—not because we were going to force those paradigms to change but so that we could see what a paradigm was in order to shift it.

Perry raised his hand. Once the shy son of a lawyer and grandson of a lawyer, he now really seemed to be in the flow of keeping the conversation going.

"I'm not sure I get it," Perry said. "When I read my notes in the health section, I see that I am thirty pounds overweight. Are you telling me not to think about counting calories and exercising or all of the self-defeating behaviors that cause me to remain at my heaviest—like eating peanut butter in the middle of the night? That I'm not supposed to dwell on these specifics?"

The presenter chuckled. "I love peanut butter! But yes, you are on the right track. Those details are important and should be part of your overall plan to evolve, but to dwell on them risks succumbing to the negative vision we discussed earlier this afternoon. Instead, I want you to embrace a new, positive vision: you as a lean, mean, fighting machine! Then, you attach positive emotions to that image and sink it into your heart so that you can generate the motivation to achieve that vision. The details will follow naturally afterward.

"That positive emotion is what I have previously called your *purpose.* When you write your new vision for each of the five areas, your purpose is one thing I want you to keep in mind. Your purpose is what ensures your follow-through, what supports you in forming certain habits and sticking to those habits. What is the emotional driver behind what you will achieve? What are the sentimental reasons that you will commit to your vision through thick and thin?

"Are you driven by your relationships? You may want to maintain an ideal weight and eat a healthy diet because you have the desire to live a long life or to be around for your children's children. You may desire longevity so that you can give back to your community or honor the sacrifices people have made for you. You may be driven by the purpose of being true to yourself.

"As you craft your new paradigms, I also want you to keep in mind your *gifts.* We are all born with natural gifts, and the best visions embody you living a life with your natural gifts in full bloom. This is often why visions don't manifest, because they aren't the right vision for you and your gifts. The vision has to fit you.

"Does anyone want to speak about one of their gifts?"

Again, Perry spoke up. It was becoming a bit of a kind-hearted running joke at our table: Now that the floodgates were open, there was no holding this man back!

"Well, I think my intuition is a gift. That's what happens when you're quiet a lot—you can hear the voice inside your own head. For example, last year my good friend Andrew . . . I knew, months before he told me, that he was going through a rough patch with his wife. I finally invited him out for coffee and offered him a means to express his feelings. He told me everything."

"A wonderful gift to have," the presenter echoed. "Now, when you are writing out your new vision, you want to make sure that vision involves using your gift of intuition. Perhaps part of the vision is to spend a certain amount of time every day being still and listening to yourself. Good advice for all of us, I believe, but especially if one of your gifts is hearing inspirations within.

"What are the gifts that the rest of you treasure about yourselves? What are you naturally good at? Are you friendship oriented? Do you enjoy laughter and having fun? Are you capable of working long hours by yourself on a project that requires detailed focus? Are you good at writing? At speaking? Organizing? Listening? Are you musical? Blessed with physical strength? You can go back to your gratitude list to see what types of activities you do that make you feel good about yourself or that others rely on you for. Jotting down a list of your gifts will help you in the vision creation process.

"Finally, when designing your future, keep in mind your *values*. Again, a vision has to conform to your values or else it will be at odds with who you really are and you won't be able to put your full weight behind it. What do you really value in life?"

The presenter stood next to my table, and I thought he was going to call on me, but he stopped by Alyse instead.

"What are you writing down there?"

Alyse smiled. "I value travel and seeing new places and new cultures, but I also value nature. And I realized that one of the reasons my travel hasn't been as fulfilling lately is because I'm working from an outdated paradigm—that travel has to be to big cities to visit art museums and go out for fancy dinners. What I really want is still to travel but to see new species of animals instead . . . to do a service trip near some of the great waterways of our world because of how much I value being outdoors."

The presenter paused dramatically, then delivered a quiet, "A-plus, Alyse. A-plus. How about the rest of you? Do you value travel and nature? Do you value quiet time to yourself to meditate and receive artistic inspiration? Do you value making a contribution to society? Family? Being honest? Earning respect? Achieving recognition? The best visions embody you living a life in which your most personal values are being honored."

The slide on the projection screen summed that up:

Purpose, Gifts & Values

I felt like I was starting to really grasp how a new vision could be formed. The presenter encouraged us to approach each of the five areas (the four quadrants plus sales) by thinking about our purpose, gifts, and values, and using them to write out what a day in our new lives could look like. *Correction, I thought to myself. What a day in my new life **will** look like.*

The presenter continued, "If you like, you can imagine that you are sitting in an easy chair and looking at a large-screen

TV presenting a film of your life. What do you see yourself doing from the time you wake up to the time you go to sleep? How will you walk through your day?

"What gifts will you use, and how? How will your purpose animate your actions? How will your values guide your actions?

"Write this out in one to two pages, and put it in the present tense. Write it as though it is happening now.

"How do you feel? What are people saying about you? Avoid using words that represent the you from the past. This is your perfect day living your ideal life. Use your senses to help bring this day alive, and state things in the positive."

One more time, Perry piped up. "Do you mean like, 'I feel so much better now that I am no longer 240 pounds'?"

"Not exactly, my friend. That's a great vision, but let's rephrase it in the positive, like this: 'I am so grateful to have achieved my perfect body weight of 210 pounds, and I can see muscles I never knew I had.'"

Our former hotshot, John, chimed in, "So, instead of saying I am happy that I am no longer in debt, I should say, 'I am so grateful to have $6,000 in my bank account for our upcoming vacation'?"

"Precisely. Do not say, 'I feel better now that I get along with a certain family member.' Instead, write about that family member and how you are enjoying the fact that you have so much in common. Perhaps you are looking forward to enjoying a special time together, when you are both excited to be in each other's company, and you feel that sense of satisfaction knowing that you are affecting someone else's life and allowing them to influence yours."

"That's exactly what I just wrote!" the mom, Cathy, exclaimed. "Well, not exactly. First, I wrote, 'I am so glad I no longer fight with my sister Krista,' but then I crossed that out and wrote, 'The bond between my sister and me is blood. We contribute so much to the world by working together.' That really does feel like a vision to me rather than just hoping the bad stuff between us will stop."

"Okay, gang," the presenter said. "You've got it down. What I want you to do now is write out a day in the life of your new vision from start to finish. Remember to include all the important areas of your life and to phrase it in the positive."

Then he left the room. I stared at my notebook, and at first the words wouldn't come. Then, I realized it was because I wasn't writing. To get the energy to do the thing, I just had to do the thing!

I turned to a new page and wrote FAMILY in big block letters across the top. I then described a perfect day for me and my family: how we speak to each other, how we support each other, what we do that brings out the best in each other, the laughter, the creativity, the learning . . .

I leaned a little bit on my best memories of our family from vacations and other relaxed times in the past, but there was plenty of new stuff, stuff that was future oriented and exciting: the things I wanted to teach my children, the way I felt when we were all in a good groove together, the way Nora and I spent our time caring for each other.

That felt great! I was excited as my hand swept across the page, now detailing my vision for my FINANCES: how everything works together, how the goals that I set come true because I am using my *gifts* (energy, relationship building, humor, leadership, and inspiration) and accomplishing my goals for the best *purpose* of expressing those gifts, namely, supporting my family and living my life as the best version of me.

The excitement naturally flowed into the area of SALES. My customers and I are engaged with each other very naturally as we both seek a progressive realization of our worthy goals. Success together!

And so on into HEALTH: I have ample energy to accomplish everything that stretches in front of me during my ideal day. I eat well, and I enjoy not only the way it prevents ailments but also how it grounds and connects me to my being.

All of this culminates in my HAPPINESS as I embody a positive attitude, resolve conflicts easily, and draw many deep breaths of gratitude during this day in my life.

By the time the presenter returned to the meeting room, I had written almost four full pages. I looked down at my handwriting, which was usually somewhat illegible, and saw that it was perhaps the clearest script I had generated in my entire life. There it was. I had my vision.

The presenter concluded the afternoon's session by telling us about the two steps left in creating our visions.

The first was spelled out on a slide:

Bring Your Vision to Life

"When you return to your hotel room or when you are back home, I want you to bring your vision to life by using pictures from magazines. Search the Internet for what you desire, and find images that stimulate an emotional reaction that says, 'That is *exactly* what I want.' Put these images in places that you will see as you go about your day."

The next slide contained the final message for the day:

Commit to Constantly Improving Your Vision

"Keep this vision alive, not only by making it appeal to the senses as you did in the previous step, but by committing in both the short term and the long term to constantly improving the script.

"In the short term you can add words that bring feeling, meaning, and emotion to the vision. What are you seeing, feeling, smelling, tasting, and hearing in the script? Bring in all of your senses.

"Can you smell the popcorn at the hockey game? Can you hear the waves crashing against the beach outside the villa? Can you see the mountains in the distance and hear the stream running down the mountainside? Can you hear the engine of the snowmobile you are buying? Can you smell its gas fumes? Can you feel the warmth of the hug from your wife or husband? Can you smell the clean air coming in through the open window as you open your eyes in the morning?

"You can also commit to improving your vision in the long term. As you begin to achieve your goals, you must remember that success is not a destination. Successful people are always striving for better. Feel the gratitude of achieving one set of goals, and at the same time, commit to adding new goals to your vision as time goes by."

Here he stopped and drew a deep breath.

"So, that's your homework." he said, and he laughed. "Rewrite your vision, and bring it to our final session tomorrow morning. Remember, you don't have to see exactly how you're going to get there, as you long as you see being there as clearly as you possibly can.

"And be open to what comes. You might be particularly focused on one quadrant right now, and that's okay. Open your mind to what you really want to do, be, and have, and don't judge what comes. Work with yourself.

"See you tomorrow!"

Chapter 8 Summary and Reflective Questions: A Vision Shift

Imagine that you are sitting in an easy chair and looking at a large-screen TV airing a film of your life. What do you see yourself doing in your ideal life from the time you wake up to the time you go to sleep?

Write this out in one to two pages, and put it in the present tense. Write it as though it is happening now.

Commit to constantly improving your vision.

DAY THREE: AM

Relaxation

When I woke up in the morning, I felt a sense of excitement that reminded me of being a young boy at the beginning of summer vacation. The day—and the world—seemed to stretch out in front of me. It was such a different feeling than I had been carrying around for the past months. In recent memory, virtually everything I laid my eyes on made me feel like a failure: I would see a bill and worry about how I was going to pay it; I would see a coworker and immediately summon up jealousy or judgment. I had been walking around expecting the worst, and in many cases, I had been getting it.

Now, I felt a lightness and a positivity that I attributed, at first, to a good night's sleep. But as I rolled onto my side and glanced at the nightstand, I realized I had barely slept at all. I had stayed up half the night writing and rewriting my vision, combining and condensing aspects so that it shrank from four pages to just over two and a half. Then I had simply rewritten that condensed version, because it felt so good to be living in this new script for my life. That was the source of my energy and optimism this morning. I was self-motivated!

I picked up my vision statement, placed it gently inside my favorite folder, tucked it into my laptop bag, and got ready to attend the last session of the seminar. At breakfast I dug out my vision statement and reread it. By then I had probably memorized it!

At one point, I peeked over the top of my document, the way one would look over the top of a newspaper, and I saw the presenter sitting at my table. I rubbed my eyes, thinking he was a vision. But no, he was there, smiling at me and dressed impeccably in a light grey suit, white shirt, and no tie.

"You didn't hear me. I didn't want to disturb you. What are you reading that's so good?"

Now it was my turn to smile. "It's my vision. I like it. I like it a lot."

We didn't speak for a few moments.

"Are you going to read our visions at some point? You know, to see if we're doing it right?"

The presenter laughed, a hearty, kind laugh. "Oh, no! I don't need to do that. I can see that you've done it right. I mean, look at you. It's in your eyes. It's in the way you're holding yourself. It's in your tone of voice. To me, you look not only ready to live your vision, but also ready to help other people find and understand theirs."

He got up from the table and extended his hand to me. After a solidly satisfying handshake he said, "We'll be in touch. I'm sure of it."

And then he was off. I made my way to the meeting room, and it was buzzing with electricity. It seemed I wasn't the only one who had produced a written vision statement to be proud of. Many attendees had theirs either clutched in their hands or discreetly displayed on their tables as if inviting others to ask about them. I sometimes have trouble feeling wholly part of a group, but I didn't this morning. This morning we were all peas in a pod.

The presenter entered from the door in the back of the room and addressed us from there.

"Today is the conclusion of our seminar. Soon you will be walking out this door, and it may be a while before we see each other again. Or it may not."

Not to sound like a rock-star groupie, but I am certain that he was looking directly at me when he said that last bit.

"It is my hope," he continued, "that our being together has occasioned the final breakthrough needed for your lasting change.

"Yesterday we learned that our attitude is what speaks to the world. The world is a reflection of our own attitudes. We determine our attitude each morning when we start our day.

"We also learned that the results we see are due to our habits. A collection of habits around a particular area of our lives is called a paradigm. We can change our paradigms one habit at a time.

"We concluded yesterday's session with the establishment of a new vision for our lives. This new, compelling vision will stir up a heightened and consistent level of self-motivation for you to go out and make your vision a reality.

"Today we will conclude the seminar with the establishment of some practices that will help you weather the storms that will surely come your way."

A slide appeared on the screen:

Relaxation

"Have you ever noticed that some of your best ideas come to you while you are on vacation, in the shower, or in the middle of the night?

"This is because your mind is at ease during these times. Effectively, your conscious mind—the part of your mind that passes judgment—is at ease, and your subconscious mind is able to do its best work. In a way it's similar to how Perry described the workings of intuition yesterday.

"I would like to suggest that you make relaxation practice a part of your daily routine. The purpose of relaxing is to help your newfound vision sink into your subconscious mind, where you can then embrace it, believe it, and be it. When you imagine yourself living your vision, it calms the mind. It shuts out all those inner voices, demands, and competing interests, in order to help ensure that your new reality blossoms.

"We don't rush anything into being. Remember, success is a *progressive realization* of a worthy ideal. In his book, *The Inner Game of Tennis*, the author W. Timothy Gallwey puts it this way:

> *When we plant a rose seed in the earth, we notice that it is small, but we do not criticize it as "rootless and stemless." We treat it as a seed, giving it the water and nourishment required of a seed. When it first shoots up out of the earth, we don't condemn it as immature and underdeveloped; nor do we criticize*

the buds for not being open when they appear. We stand in wonder at the process taking place and give the plant the care and nourishment it needs at each stage of its development. The rose is a rose from the time it is a seed to the time it dies. Within it, at all times, it contains its whole potential. It seems to be constantly in the process of change; yet at each state, at each moment, it is perfectly all right as it is.

"That is another great way to reconnect with your subconscious mind: to witness the growth of a plant or just to get out in nature in general, like Alyse was talking about. In nature we get to experience firsthand that animals are not sidetracked by a conscious mind. We get to be one with the world around us, to feel at ease. Nature is a great place to quiet the mind and let our vision settle, as Alyse was reminding us.

"My favorite place to settle myself into a very relaxed state is on our living room sofa. No offense, Alyse! I just lie there and release any tension in my muscles. I create an image in my mind of a log cabin in the country. The fire is blazing, and I can hear the crackling of the wood. There is a light snow coming down outside. The trees are covered in snow. I am sitting in a reclining chair and looking out a large window. To the right is a hill, and to the left is a slow-moving stream. Once I get myself to this point in the visualization process, I begin to think about the areas of my life—family, finances, sales, health, and happiness—and I visualize myself being and doing things in a way that I know will attract the results I desire.

"What are some other ways you can let your newfound vision settle in?"

Bill's wife, Judy, raised her hand.

"Well, I work in real estate, as some of you know by now. When I have an important appointment to show a house, I go to a coffee shop near the house. I try to get there half an hour early. And by that, I mean a real half hour, like I already have my latte—"

Someone near Judy chuckled, and she responded in mock offense, "What, you don't think an older lady like me knows how to order a latte? Anyway, I make sure I am seated before the golden half hour begins. At that time, I don't consciously think about the prospective buyer or how important the deal is or might be. Instead, I read something inspiring or write in my journal. My one rule is that, whatever I do, I let the thoughts come. I don't ever force them.

"Then, when I'm ready to leave, I find that I have centered myself. I'm ready for whatever comes from the appointment. I'm aware that things will be as they are supposed to be."

We were all a little stunned by this practice coming out of such a meek-looking, elderly woman. Seeing our silence, she added, somewhat unnecessarily, "Does that make sense?"

The presenter thundered, "Exactly! So much sense. You have just demonstrated how well relaxation applies to the selling experience. Keep in mind that the way consumers buy, whether they are homeowners or business decision makers, has changed dramatically. Two forces are pushing this change: the Internet and the evolution of the human psyche.

"The Internet, because of its ever-increasing, rich content, provides an avenue for buyers to educate themselves on their own terms. In your case, they might show up already knowing the comparable houses that have recently sold in the area, the rankings of the various school districts, or the local taxes. You aren't the one informing them about these things, am I right?"

Judy nodded emphatically.

"In your case, but really for all of us, the buyer is now armed with enough data to make their own decision. This has caused the human psyche to evolve, so traditional approaches to selling, such as channeling the buyer down a path using your own agenda, will only put up an immediate wall in the minds of buyers.

"When you spend your time relaxing, you are doing nothing short of visualizing yourself as a modern-day sales professional. A modern-day sales professional is just that, a professional. A modern-day sales professional helps people identify and solve their problems."

Chapter 9 Summary and Reflective Questions: Relaxation

Have you ever noticed that some of your best ideas come to you while you are on vacation, in the shower, or in the middle of the night? This is because your mind is at ease during these times.

Will you dedicate time each day to relaxing so your new vision will take root? When will you do this?

Self-Doubt

After a short break, we reassembled in the meeting room for what I thought would be the last time, until a tablemate of mine looked at the schedule and confirmed we had two short sessions left rather than just one.

The presenter was bent over his desk. At first, it looked like he was searching for a contact lens, but then I realized he was just head-down on the desk.

Nobody spoke for a while. In an effort to lighten the mood, I eventually said, "Is it nap time?"

"I can't do it," the presenter said, in a kind of a moan, "I can't do it. . . ."

It was hard to make out his words, because his face was turned to one side. "The first things I tried to do to make my vision a reality didn't work out. Now I'm back home, and the buzz from the seminar has worn off, and I'm right back where I started. Aren't I?"

He then sat bolt upright in his chair. "This will happen to you," he warned. "You might leave a seminar like this feeling pumped and running on an emotional high. Three days later, though, you will be tempted to slip back into living life based on your preexisting programming. You will hit a wall, and fear will overtake your images of freedom. Your old paradigms will creep back in, and bam, you're back to square one!

"I want to bring this to your attention, because I would feel remiss if I didn't. When self-doubt hits you, identify it. Don't let it push you away from your vision. Remind yourself that your present results are indicators of your past vision and that the only way to break the cycle is to stay true to yourself and the new vision you have for your life.

"When we decide to use our freedom, to act on a new idea, it is natural to have doubts that the new idea will become reality. This produces a feeling of fear. That negative vision that picks up on little bumps in the road creates anxiety. We then go back to our old paradigms. When we succumb to self-doubt in this way, we lose track of our vision, and our subconscious can't produce a new set of results for us. We have, in effect, sabotaged ourselves."

I'm sure my face turned ghastly white at the thought!

The presenter continued, "When these fears come to your mind, and they will, imagine writing them out on a piece of paper and burning the paper. I used to actually do this in the seminar, but one time it set off the smoke alarms. The piercing sound alerted hotel security, and I had to talk my way back into being able to use that conference center again—" The crowd laughed at this thought. "So now I just suggest that you set fire to your fears in your mind . . . or at least outside. By doing this you slowly but surely reinforce your new beliefs and habits.

"Remember, to change the color of a piece of cloth you must soak the cloth in dye and let it dry. Depending on how dark you want the color, you must do this hundreds of times.

"Or you can think of it this way: How many of you in this room love roller coasters?"

About half of the participants raised their hands.

Bill muttered something about not being able to stand roller coasters ever since his mom told him about an accident that had happened at one of the first major theme parks ever built in the area where he grew up.

The presenter asked him to share the story with the group.

"Oh, this was before you were all born. I think it might even have still been made out of wood."

"Okay, exactly." The presenter smiled. "The source of your fear is past conditioning, but that conditioning is out of date. Roller coasters are made out of reinforced steel now, with advanced computer sensors as part of the safety system. We all need to update our paradigms, and this is just one example. Is it okay for me to continue with the roller coaster example, Bill?"

Bill laughed and nodded his assent.

"Well, life is often a roller coaster. The only question is the attitude with which you commit to it.

"Let's say the excitement of the ride represents freedom. But between the time you get the idea to go on the roller coaster and when your ride actually begins, there is a long line. This line provides ample opportunity for you to chicken out and let fear stand in the way of freedom.

"Again, freedom is the fun and the feeling of accomplishment you will have during the ride and afterward. Once you board the roller coaster, you are in; you cannot be on it halfway. Will you let fear cause you to run away from the roller coaster before the ride even starts?

"You are now poised to move on to a more satisfying, purpose-driven life. If you get caught by something from your past, repeat this statement to yourself: 'You make mistakes; mistakes don't make you.'

"Line up for the roller coaster, have faith, and trust. And remember, the universe is there to support you. Things will fall into place, and your worst fears will not come true. You may have setbacks, but none that you cannot overcome. And overcome them you will."

Chapter 10 Summary and Reflective Questions: Self-Doubt

When self-doubt hits you, identify it. Don't let it push you away from your vision.

Remind yourself that your present results are indicators of your past vision and that the only way to break the cycle is to stay true to yourself and the new vision you have for your life.

You are now poised to move on to a more satisfying, purpose-driven life.

If you become caught by something from your past, repeat this statement to yourself: "You make mistakes; mistakes don't make you."

Affirmations

As we all returned to the meeting room for the final session, I felt a little sad. This had been such an uplifting experience, but was the presenter right? Would I be like one of those attendees who, three days later, flamed out and was back listening to negative internal messages and recreating poor results from faulty paradigms?

Displaying his magic touch one final time, the presenter asked us to look back over the gratitude list we had made on the first afternoon of the workshop. As I pored over my list, I found so many things I didn't even remember writing, things that made me say to myself, *That's right!* or *And that, too, I am grateful for!*

The presenter resumed his place behind the lectern and changed the slide:

Affirmations

A reflexive groan went up from the audience. The presenter smiled.

"I know, I know. Affirmations. Those 'I' statements phrased in the present tense but that anticipate the future. Like, 'I make good decisions that move me toward my ideals.' I acknowledge that a sentence in that form doesn't seem natural. But even though it often gets a bad rap—much like gratitude does—I would like to conclude our seminar with the topic of affirmations. Affirmations in circles of New Thought have been overpublicized, overplayed, and misunderstood.

"Let me make one thing clear. We are not using affirmations to hypnotize the subconscious mind into feeling that it can have or do something that isn't meant for it. Affirmations are not ego-driven thoughts, nor are they about comparing yourself to an outside influence. Instead, affirmations are framed as purpose-driven. They are about us being true to a vision based on our values and our gifts. They are authentic to us. They may sound a little strange at first, but affirmations are the most powerful way for us to transplant new and necessary beliefs and habits into our subconscious mind so that we can achieve our newly defined vision.

"The best affirmations are focused on your independent destiny and show you moving toward your worthy ideal. I'll give you a few examples of mine.

"I treat my mind and body with the respect they deserve.

"I deserve and welcome progressive success into my life.

"I bring immense value to my clients by helping them realize their hearts' desires.

"These affirmations are based on what I am doing and are grounded in my personal reasons for doing it. If it helps you create affirmations that are right for you, you can consider them through the lens of character traits. What traits do you need in order to achieve your vision?

"You might say, 'I am a problem solver' or 'I am a creative thinker.' You can also reflect on your gifts and your values in order to craft affirmations, such as, 'I write 1,000 words per day to improve my craft' or 'I focus on the most important things that I need to do today.'

"Finally, the best affirmations are in the form of a sentence that helps you create the future by affirming a specific belief to your subconscious mind. In this way you are attracting to yourself what you *need* in order to get what you *want*. Does anyone want to volunteer an example?"

One of my tablemates, Alex, who hadn't participated very much to this point, raised his hand. "Well, I almost feel sheepish to say this, but I have a recording on my smartphone in my own voice. As I drive around town, I turn on a recording of me reading my affirmations—"

"Can we hear it?" the presenter asked.

Alex was stunned. "Um, what?"

"Can we hear your recording? I think we're all on the same team by now. Right, gang? And we are far past judgment."

Alex looked like he wished that he hadn't opened his mouth, and I didn't blame him. Nonetheless, he rose and approached the microphone at the lectern. He opened the application on his phone and, closing one eye in a kind of exaggerated wince, he pressed play.

"I am enthusiastic, and it is contagious," the recording began. "I laugh and love every day. I am cool, calm, and collected. Money is flowing to me in abundance through multiple streams of income. I make decisions quickly and stay true to my word. I take care of my mind and body. I save ten percent of my income. I treat my family with the respect they deserve. I make time for fun every day."

The presenter laid his hand on Alex's shoulder. "That is utterly fantastic, my friend. This is exactly what we all need to do next. Craft a series of affirmations in the wonderfully inspired fashion you have just heard here. Perhaps, like Alex, you will also record them on your smartphone and let yourself hear your own wisdom as you communicate directly with your subconscious."

When I first tried to write some affirmations, I felt a little bit stuck. *Hey,* I chuckled to myself, *maybe Alex had already taken all of the good ones!* But then I got the hang of it and came up with some good ones myself:

- *I wake up each morning one hour before the rest of my family.*

- *I exercise vigorously for sixty minutes three times per week and leisurely for forty minutes two times per week.*

- *I surround myself with success-minded people.*

- *My relationships with my children are growing stronger every day. They are inspired by me, and I love them very much.*

- *Nora and I are in love. We support and care for each other.*

- *I welcome freedom and independence into my world.*

I was mid-thought when the presenter drew the seminar to a close. "A good affirmation is exactly what I want for each of you—for all of us—and I can think of no better way to close this seminar than by sharing with you a few more of mine. My hope is that you will use them and that they will keep you company as you watch your thoughts and your world evolve.

"I focus on the positive.

"I am enjoying the fruits of cause and effect.

"I am an inspiration to others, helping them to make the most of themselves.

"I am working with infinite supply.

"I am a creator of value.

"I love my life. Life loves me.

The presenter paused one last moment, and then simply said: "Thank you very much."

And, with that, the seminar was over.

Chapter 11 Summary and Reflective Questions: Affirmations

Affirmations are framed as purpose-driven. They are about you being true to a vision that is based on your values and your gifts.

Affirmations may sound a little strange at first, but they are the most powerful way for you to transplant new and necessary beliefs and habits into your subconscious mind so that you can achieve your newly defined vision.

What are five affirmations that reflect your new vision?

CONCLUSION

The return to reality wasn't nearly as bad as I had thought it would be. The few times I had thought about my job during the seminar had prompted feelings of dread: not *that* boss, not *that* approach to sales, I don't think I can *take* it any longer. But when the seminar ended, I found myself in a brighter, happier place. I was completing my gratitude list and crafting some well-turned affirmations just before dawn each morning. It seemed that just as I finished my journaling each day the birds began to sing.

I went forth in my daily life with a new, positive attitude showing in my face, and people around me reacted to that attitude. I noticed the change the day the seminar ended. One of my most vivid memories of that time is of driving back to Winnipeg to catch my flight home. Along the way I stopped at a shopping mall in Grand Forks, North Dakota, and as I walked through the mall I noticed people smiling at me. My gratitude and confidence was bringing joy to the world around me, and I saw that joy reflected on the faces around me. I wasn't going to stop now.

When I returned to work, I said to myself, I'm going to take control here. I'm not going to quit my job; instead, I'm going to find a way around my boss and transform my role in the company. I started to forge a relationship with the ownership of the company so that I could show the owners that the sales approach we were taking was not the way professional services are supposed to be sold.

While those relationships were being built and strengthened, I also turned my focus inward. During the seminar, whenever the presenter talked about success being the progressive realization of a worthy ideal, one image seemed to always pop into my head: I wanted to build a cottage that my family and I could enjoy. I could see the cottage and its surroundings: the lake, the loons, the social life, the fun we would have as a family . . . Nora and I relaxing on a Saturday afternoon and playing board games with the kids or reading, with the fire roaring and snow coming down outside. . . a place my mom and dad could enjoy as they grew older. After all, they had sacrificed so much to get me to where I was now—it was time for me to start giving back to them. The cottage would have three bedrooms, a loft, a wraparound deck, and a garage. I originally wrote out this vision as part of the seminar assignment, but afterward I remembered to study that goal every day. It was the picture I set in my mind.

I didn't know where the money to complete this vision would come from. I didn't know how I'd find the time to oversee the cottage's construction or even where the land would be located. We had a favorite lake in Newfoundland where some of our friends had cottages, but all of the waterfront property there had already been purchased. I could hear the presenter's voice in my head reminding me that I was looking at things the wrong way. If I simply looked at how much it was going to cost and compared that to what I was making right now, I would talk myself out of it. Instead of thinking of all the reasons why it couldn't happen, I focused on making the vision clear. I experienced the vision. I embraced the vision. I communicated with my subconscious about the vision and then followed the signs toward making the vision come true.

I remembered the presenter also telling us that you cannot expect to just wake up and be in possession of the worthy ideal. You need to avoid the self-sabotage that old paradigms would try to instigate by instead planting new paradigms in your mind. 'I cannot afford a second home' became 'I deserve a cottage.' 'I have never built a cottage before' became 'I can build a cottage. I have the support of friends who have been there and done that.'

Most people spend time desiring what they think they can get rather than what they really want. As I reflected deeply on my true desires, the changes at work became more pronounced. The owners began to see that viewing sales as a numbers game, in which salespeople met as many people as they could in order to fill their quotas, did not build customer loyalty, retention, or referrals.

Instead, they started to believe in the approach to selling that I was touting, in which the relationship is the most important part. Even if the sales cycle was a little longer, finding solutions to the problems that our customers actually possessed had long lasting results for the overall health of the business in terms of referrals and positive word of mouth.

My boss was dismissed, and I was promoted to Vice President of Sales. I didn't feel any joy in my boss being let go. My take on it was simply that it had to happen in order for him to realize that his way of doing business wasn't working. The last I heard he had landed in another organization and had a more positive approach toward working with others.

In the two years since I completed the *It's Time to Sell* seminar, the aspects of my life that I included in my regular, recurring vision have started to take shape. That lake where all of the waterfront properties had been purchased? Well, it turns out that one parcel of land had been reserved for a couple who later left the area to pursue a business opportunity many miles away. It came available for sale, and I jumped on it.

Once I had decided on my worthy ideal, I broke its accomplishment into steps or goals. After we secured the land, I spoke to a friend of mine and documented all the steps he had gone through to get his cottage built. Nora and I worked with an architect on the drawings. We hired someone to clear the lot, a contractor to frame the cottage, and so on.

My point is that I didn't achieve the vision of having a cottage overnight. However, by staying true to the vision, by applying these principles, and by following through with action, I was able to face and conquer apparent impossibilities. I could never have foreseen the size of the raise that I would receive for being true to relationship selling. My family is certainly glad I stuck with that approach, though—perhaps most of all my dog, who at this moment is nestled, dreaming, by my feet in front of the fire at the cottage as I pen the final words of this book.

What will the future hold? I now believe, as strongly as I believe that the sky is blue, that I can achieve every goal on my list that is right for me. Each goal I accomplish will be replaced by new, more exciting ones.

One of my favorite aspects of my unfolding vision is my recent desire to give back in the form of sales mentorship. I think the presenter first predicted this when he cryptically told me that we would meet again someday. I don't know whether he meant that figuratively or literally. Time will tell!

In the meantime, the great relationships I have with my family, my customers, my community, and myself bring me much joy. And I know that the future will be even better, bigger, and brighter.

About the Author

Chris is an entrepreneur and sales expert. After consciously choosing the sales profession as a means to create a better life for himself and his family, he found negative images of sales cropping up in his mind and holding him back. He decided to conquer the negative images and transform them to serve him better. Following this mind-set shift, Chris was able to discover and use his innate values and gifts to become a top sales professional. Chris inspires entrepreneurs and sales professionals to deal with paradigms that hold them back from getting their products or services to market. Go to www.chrisspurvey.com to continue your journey, and download the free workbook companion to this book.

Made in the USA
Coppell, TX
08 June 2021